Other books by Randy Lariscy:

Portraits of Forgiveness –
Finding the Inspiration and Courage to Forgive

Insight Bible Commentary –
The Book of Mark (Volume 1)

The Evangelism Engine –
*Build a Sustainable Evangelism Ministry
in Your Church
(Coming in 2013)*

SPEEDY DEVOTIONS

Volume 1 - Wise Choices

Concise Thoughts With Life-Changing Impact

Randy Lariscy

WordTruth Press℠
USA

1st Edition published by **WordTruth Press**ˢᴹ in the United States (SAN: 920-2811). Find us on the web at WordTruthPress.com. You can contact WordTruth Press by phone at 404.919.WORD (9673) or by email at Info@WordTruthPress.com.

ISBN-13: 978-0-9852899-2-8
Library of Congress Control Number: 2012944507

Acknowledgements

*Dedicated to my lovely wife –
and to everyone else who has a hard time
reading a book without pictures.*

Contents

Study Guide

Speedy Devotions is intended for people who think they have little time to study the Bible. The Bible can certainly be intimidating in its size and scope. Many find it hard to stay focused on long passages of Scripture. Yet the Bible is God's word for all people. And even a small amount of God's word can have a profound impact on your life.

In volume one, Speedy Devotions will focus on wise choices. The book of Proverbs, more than any other single book, contains practical guidance on how to live the kind of life that God desires. It provides startling insights into human behavior along with God's perspective on how best to live and relate to people.

The format of this devotional is simple. Each day you will encounter:

- **God's Word**: Only one or two Bible verses to consider.
- **Life Principle**: A short thought based God's word to help you understand the key teaching.
- **Life Change**: Space to reflect and record the life change you need to make.

The last step does not need to take a long time – but it is the most critical part of the process. As the Bible teaches, "**Do not merely listen to the word, and so deceive yourselves. Do what it says**" (James 1:22, NIV). Whether you spend five minutes or five hours studying the Bible, it will not matter unless you adjust your attitude or actions based on the teaching from God's word.

Think about specific ways to apply the teaching to your life. As you consider the life change you need to make, these symbols will appear each day to remind you of the possible applications:

Symbol	Application
⇨	A command to follow
∞	A principle to use
💭	Thoughts to engage and attitudes to avoid
📢	What you say and how you say it
⚒	A good work to start
✦	A sin to confess and forsake
🎯	Thanksgiving for God's hand at work in your life

Take the time – just a little time – to spend some quality moments with God in

His word. Really listen to what He is saying to you. And then follow Him. It is a simple but life-changing process.

Have no fear about making these changes. The LORD said, "**I have come that they may have life, and have it to the full**" (John 10:10, NIV). The life the LORD Jesus desires for you is really the only life worth living.

January

> *The proverbs of Solomon son of David,*
> *king of Israel: for attaining wisdom...*
> *(Proverbs 1:1-2, NIV)*

Symbol	Life Change
⇨	A command to follow
∞	A principle to use
💭	Thoughts to engage and attitudes to avoid
📢	What you say and how you say it
⚒	A good work to start
✠	A sin to confess and forsake
🎯	Thanksgiving for God's hand at work in your life

January 1

God's Word	*The fear of the LORD is the beginning of knowledge, but fools despise wisdom and discipline. (Proverbs 1:7, NIV)*
Life Principle	It is the LORD God who created your world. The knowledge of living well in His world must come from His word. Are you prepared live life on His terms?
Life changes	_____ _____ _____ _____ _____ _____ _____ _____

January 2

God's Word	...the complacency of fools will destroy them; but whoever listens to Me will live in safety and be at ease, without fear of harm. (Proverbs 1:32-33, NIV)
Life Principle	If you hear and obey the wisdom of God, you can live with confidence and security. No fear of evil and no dread of doom.
Life changes	_____ _____ _____ _____ _____ _____ _____ _____

January 3

God's Word	*If you ... search for it as for hidden treasure, then you will understand the fear of the LORD and find the knowledge of God. (Proverbs 2:4-5, NIV)*
Life Principle	God's wisdom is accessible. But you must diligently search for it as you would a hidden treasure. Study the Bible, meditate on His truth, do what He commands.
Life changes	_____ _____ _____ _____ _____ _____ _____

January 4

God's Word	*For he guards the course of the just and protects the way of his faithful ones. Then you will understand what is right and just and fair-every good path. (Proverbs 2:8-9, NIV)*
Life Principle	Integrity is the key to understanding all that is good. Until you live with integrity, you will view every person and situation with a dark cloud.
Life changes	_____ _____ _____ _____ _____ _____ _____

January 5

God's Word	*My son, do not forget my teaching, but keep my commands in your heart, for they will prolong your life many years ...* *(Proverbs 3:1-2, NIV)*
Life Principle	Do not miss life's most important lesson: walk with God. You cannot add a single day to your life but, through foolishness, you can cut it short.
Life changes	_____ _____ _____ _____ _____ _____ _____

January 6

God's Word	*Trust in the LORD with all your heart and lean not on your own understanding; in all your ways acknowledge him ...* *(Proverbs 3:5-6, NIV)*
Life Principle	It is a long, crooked road in life when you follow your own path. Trust God. Trust His word. Put your faith in Him. And He will straighten that crooked road.
Life changes	_____ _____ _____ _____ _____ _____ _____ _____

January 7

God's Word	*Do not be wise in your own eyes; fear the LORD and shun evil. This will bring health to your body and nourishment to your bones.* *(Proverbs 3:7-8, NIV)*
Life Principle	The LORD was doing just fine before you arrived and He will do just fine when you are gone. Stop trying to do things your own way and get with His program.
Life changes	_____ _____ _____ _____ _____ _____ _____ _____

January 8

God's Word	*Honor the LORD with your wealth, with the firstfruits of all your crops; then your barns will be filled to overflowing ...* *(Proverbs 3:9-10, NIV)*
Life Principle	Give the LORD your first and He will give you His best.
Life changes	_____ _____ _____ _____ _____ _____ _____ _____

January 9

God's Word	*Do not withhold good from those who deserve it, when it is in your power to act. (Proverbs 3:27-28, NIV)*
Life Principle	There is no shame in saying "No" when you are unable to help. Yet you must DO the good that you ARE able to do WHEN you are able to do it. Later may be too late.
Life changes	_____ _____ _____ _____ _____ _____ _____ ⇨ ∞ 💭 ◁ 👆 ⊕ 🎯

January 10

God's Word	*Wisdom is supreme; therefore get wisdom. Though it cost all you have, get understanding. Esteem her, and she will exalt you... (Proverbs 4:7-8, NIV)*
Life Principle	Understanding life can only come from God. The last thing you will want is to give an account of your life to God without the faintest idea of what it all meant.
Life changes	_____ _____ _____ _____ _____ _____ _____ _____

January 11

God's Word	*I guide you in the way of wisdom and lead you along straight paths. When you walk, your steps will not be hampered ...* (Proverbs 4:11-12, NIV)
Life Principle	Life is unsteady when you cannot see the path ahead. Every step is calculated yet unsure. Let God direct your path and you can fly like the wind.
Life changes	_____ _____ _____ _____ _____ _____ _____

January 12

God's Word	*Listen closely to my words ..., keep them within your heart; for they are life to those who find them and health to [your] whole body. (Proverbs 4:20-22, NIV)*
Life Principle	Obeying God with passion is healthier than disobeying Him with apathy.
Life changes	

January 13

God's Word	*Above all else, guard your heart, for it is the wellspring of life. (Proverbs 4:23, NIV)*
Life Principle	Guard your thought life from any deceit or perversity. All of life's problems begin with a single, crooked thought.
Life changes	_____ _____ _____ _____ _____ _____ _____ ⇨ ∞ 💭 ◁ 👆 ⊕ 🎯

January 14

God's Word	Drink water from your own cistern, running water from your own well. (Proverbs 5:15, NIV)
Life Principle	God will give you plenty. There is no need to take from another.
Life changes	

January 15

God's Word	*May you rejoice in the wife of your youth ... may her breasts satisfy you always, may you ever be captivated by her love.* *(Proverbs 5:18-19, NIV)*
Life Principle	By His own design for marriage, God is able to satisfy one man with one woman for an entire lifetime.
Life changes	_____ _____ _____ _____ _____ _____ _____ ⇨ ∞ 💭 📢 ☝ ⊕ 🎯

January 16

God's Word	For a man's ways are in full view of the LORD, and He examines all his paths. (Proverbs 5:21, NIV)
Life Principle	God is watching over you. And He knows every path you take, every thought you think, and every idle word you speak. If you forget this truth, you will go astray.
Life changes	_____ _____ _____ _____ _____ _____ _____ _____

January 17

God's Word	*If you have put up security for your neighbor ... then do this ... to free yourself ... humble yourself; press your plea with your neighbor! (Proverbs 6:1,3, NIV)*
Life Principle	Never guarantee the payment of another person. Instead, give them whatever you are able to give with no strings attached. You will sleep much better.
Life changes	_____ _____ _____ _____ _____ _____ _____

January 18

God's Word	*Go to the ant, you sluggard; consider its ways ... It has no commander ... yet it stores its provisions in summer and gathers its food at harvest. (Proverbs 6:6-8, NIV)*
Life Principle	Laziness begins when you hit the 'Snooze' button on your alarm clock. A righteous person will not be lazy!
Life changes	_____ _____ _____ _____ _____ _____ _____

January 19

God's Word	*A scoundrel and villain ... who plots evil with deceit in his heart ... disaster will overtake him in an instant; he will suddenly be destroyed. (Proverbs 6:12,14-15, NIV)*
Life Principle	If you continue to devise evil plans in your mind, you will certainly deceive others in your life. God will not be deceived – He will ensure you reap what you sow.
Life changes	_____ _____ _____ _____ _____ _____ _____ _____

January 20

God's Word	*There are six things the LORD hates, seven that are detestable to him... (Proverbs 6:16, NIV)*
Life Principle	God loves people. Yet He hates sin. Here are seven to avoid: arrogant pride, lying, murder, evil plans, evil actions, perjury, and divisiveness.
Life changes	_____ _____ _____ _____ _____ _____ _____ _____

January 21

God's Word	*Bind them upon your heart forever; fasten them around your neck. When you walk, they will guide you ... when you awake, they will speak to you. (Proverbs 6:21-22, NIV)*
Life Principle	When you plant the seeds of God's truth in your mind, they continue to bear good fruit in your life. God's commands will come to mind at just the right time.
Life changes	_____ _____ _____ _____ _____ _____ _____ _____

January 22

God's Word	*Men do not despise a thief if he steals to satisfy his hunger. But a man who commits adultery lacks judgment ...* *(Proverbs 6:30,32, NIV)*
Life Principle	One can understand a man who steals a loaf of bread because he is hungry. But a man who steals his neighbor's wife can never repay the debt.
Life changes	_____ _____ _____ _____ _____ _____ _____ _____

January 23

God's Word	*Keep my commands and you will live; guard my teachings as the apple of your eye ... they will keep you from the adulteress... (Proverbs 7:1-2,5, NIV)*
Life Principle	Love for the word of God will overcome lust in the heart.
Life changes	_____ _____ _____ _____ _____ _____ _____ ⇨ ∞ 🗩 ◁ ☝ ⊕ 🎯

January 24

God's Word	*I, wisdom, dwell together with prudence; I possess knowledge and discretion. (Proverbs 8:12, NIV)*
Life Principle	A wise person deals with people using prudence and discretion in all matters. No need to embarrass anyone – show the consideration you would want for yourself.
Life changes	_____ _____ _____ _____ _____ _____ _____ _____

January 25

God's Word	*I walk in the way of righteousness, along the paths of justice, bestowing wealth on those who love me and making their treasuries full. (Proverbs 8:20-21, NIV)*
Life Principle	Walking in righteousness assures you of great riches - not material wealth but even better. You gain strength of character and contentment in all things.
Life changes	_____ _____ _____ _____ _____ _____ _____

January 26

God's Word	*Blessed are those who keep my ways ... Blessed is the man who listens to me, watching daily at my doors, waiting at my doorway. (Proverbs 8:32,34, NIV)*
Life Principle	To be wise you must pursue God's wisdom: listening to His word, watching for His work, waiting for His presence, and walking in His ways.
Life changes	_____ _____ _____ _____ _____ _____ _____

January 27

God's Word	*For whoever finds me finds life and receives favor from the LORD. But whoever fails to find me harms himself; all who hate me love death. (Proverbs 8:35-36, NIV)*
Life Principle	Two paths in this world: The pursuit of God's wisdom bringing life and God's favor; the rejection of God's wisdom, bringing harm to yourself. Choose…
Life changes	_____ _____ _____ _____ _____ _____ _____ _____

January 28

God's Word	*Whoever corrects a mocker invites insult ... Do not rebuke a mocker or he will hate you; rebuke a wise man and he will love you. (Proverbs 9:7-8, NIV)*
Life Principle	You cannot expect that correcting a scoffer will gain his praise. He will hate your correction and hate you too.
Life changes	

January 29

God's Word	*Instruct a wise man and he will be wiser still; teach a righteous man and he will add to his learning. (Proverbs 9:9, NIV)*
Life Principle	Never fear correcting a righteous person who errs. A righteous person has a teachable spirit and will only grow wiser.
Life changes	_____ _____ _____ _____ _____ _____ _____

January 30

God's Word	*The fear of the LORD is the beginning of wisdom ... For through me your days will be many, and years will be added to your life. (Proverbs 9:10-11, NIV)*
Life Principle	Nothing in this world can make sense without the foundational truths that God is, that God created all things, and that you are accountable to Him.
Life changes	_____ _____ _____ _____ _____ _____ _____ _____

January 31

God's Word	*If you are wise, your wisdom will reward you; if you are a mocker, you alone will suffer. (Proverbs 9:12, NIV)*
Life Principle	You have a choice: be wise or be foolish. The consequences will fall on you either way.
Life changes	_____ _____ _____ _____ _____ _____ _____

February

> The proverbs of Solomon
> son of David, king of Israel:
> for attaining ... discipline...
> (Proverbs 1:1-2, NIV)

Symbol	Life Change
⇨	A command to follow
∞	A principle to use
💭	Thoughts to engage and attitudes to avoid
📢	What you say and how you say it
⚒	A good work to start
✛	A sin to confess and forsake
🎯	Thanksgiving for God's hand at work in your life

February 1

God's Word	*The woman Folly is loud; she is undisciplined and without knowledge ... her guests are in the depths of the grave. (Proverbs 9:13,18, NIV)*
Life Principle	How does a person become foolish? Ignore God's word. Focus on yourself and on the now. Start thinking that anything is OK as long as you do not get caught.
Life changes	_____ _____ _____ _____ _____ _____ _____

February 2

God's Word	*Ill-gotten treasures are of no value, but righteousness delivers from death. (Proverbs 10:2, NIV)*
Life Principle	Wealth earned by pure motives and hard work can be enjoyed while ill-gotten treasure brings no profit at all.
Life changes	_____ _____ _____ _____ _____ _____ _____ _____

February 3

God's Word	*The LORD does not let the righteous go hungry but he thwarts the craving of the wicked.* *(Proverbs 10:3, NIV)*
Life Principle	Better to be poor and righteous than rich and wicked. The hunger of the righteous will be satisfied.
Life changes	_____ _____ _____ _____ _____ _____ _____

February 4

God's Word	*Lazy hands make a man, but diligent hands bring wealth. (Proverbs 10:4, NIV)*
Life Principle	You have to work to make money; it is just that simple.
Life changes	_____ _____ _____ _____ _____ _____ _____ _____

February 5

God's Word	*He who gathers crops in summer is a wise son, but he who sleeps during harvest is a disgraceful son.* *(Proverbs 10:5, NIV)*
Life Principle	Do what you can, while you can, as well as you can, for as long as you can.
Life changes	_____ _____ _____ _____ _____ _____ _____

February 6

God's Word	*The memory of the righteous will be a blessing, but the name of the wicked will rot. (Proverbs 10:7, NIV)*
Life Principle	What will people say about you when you are gone? You establish your legacy in the now.
Life changes	_____ _____ _____ _____ _____ _____ _____ _____

February 7

God's Word	*The wise in heart accept commands, but a chattering fool comes to ruin. (Proverbs 10:8, NIV)*
Life Principle	God gave us two ears and only one mouth for a reason – so you can "wise up."
Life changes	_____ _____ _____ _____ _____ _____ _____

February 8

God's Word	*The man of integrity walks securely, but he who takes crooked paths will be found out.* *(Proverbs 10:9, NIV)*
Life Principle	If you want to get a good night's sleep, stick with the truth. Lies will eventually be found out.
Life changes	

February 9

God's Word	*The mouth of the righteous is a fountain of life, but violence overwhelms the mouth of the wicked. (Proverbs 10:11, NIV)*
Life Principle	The words you speak can be a life-giving fountain of hope, encouragement, and refreshment to others. Do not allow angry words to quench that fountain.
Life changes	_____ _____ _____ _____ _____ _____ _____

February 10

God's Word	Hatred stirs up dissension, but love covers over all wrongs. (Proverbs 10:12, NIV)
Life Principle	There are many minor offenses in life that can and should be overlooked in love. Otherwise, you will lead a miserable life, one full of conflict.
Life changes	_____ _____ _____ _____ _____ _____ _____

February 11

God's Word	*Wisdom is found on the lips of the discerning, but a rod is for the back of him who lacks judgment. (Proverbs 10:13, NIV)*
Life Principle	Think before you speak. Is it accurate? Check your facts. Is it biblical? Check your bible. Is it helpful? Check you motives. Is it sensitive? Check your humility.
Life changes	_____ _____ _____ _____ _____ _____ _____

February 12

God's Word	*Wise men store up knowledge, but the mouth of a fool invites ruin. (Proverbs 10:14, NIV)*
Life Principle	Spend less time talking and more time learning. The only way to prepare for what lies ahead is to learn today.
Life changes	

February 13

God's Word	*The wages of the righteous bring them life ... He who heeds discipline shows the way to life ... (Proverbs 10:16-17, NIV)*
Life Principle	Walk with God and you will never be lost. Along the way, you will help many people experience the same blessings you enjoy on the path to abundant life.
Life changes	_____ _____ _____ _____ _____ _____ _____

February 14

God's Word	*When words are many, sin is not absent, but he who holds his tongue is wise.* *(Proverbs 10:19, NIV)*
Life Principle	Learn to limit your words to the needs of the listener. You can say a little, or say a lot. Just do not say too much
Life changes	_____ _____ _____ _____ _____ _____ _____ ⇨ ∞ 🗨 📢 ⛪ ⊕ 🎯

February 15

God's Word	*The blessing of the LORD brings wealth, and He adds no trouble to it. (Proverbs 10:22, NIV)*
Life Principle	True riches are not found in money but in the blessing of the LORD. Money can be spent or lost but God's love, joy, peace, provision, and posterity last forever.
Life changes	_____ _____ _____ _____ _____ _____ _____

February 16

God's Word	*The prospect of the righteous is joy, but the hopes of the wicked come to nothing. (Proverbs 10:28, NIV)*
Life Principle	When you trust in the LORD Jesus, you live with the confident expectation of your home in Heaven and Jesus welcoming you there!
Life changes	_____ _____ _____ _____ _____ _____ _____

February 17

God's Word	*The mouth of the righteous brings forth wisdom, but a perverse tongue will be cut out.* *(Proverbs 10:31, NIV)*
Life Principle	The one who listens to God becomes wise, learning to say what is right and appropriate. There is coming a day when God will silence corrupt words.
Life changes	_____ _____ _____ _____ _____ _____ _____

February 18

God's Word	*The LORD abhors dishonest scales, but accurate weights are his delight.* *(Proverbs 11:1, NIV)*
Life Principle	To please the LORD, you must treat others with honesty and fairness, just as you want them to treat you. Cheating is detestable to the LORD.
Life changes	_____ _____ _____ _____ _____ _____ _____ _____

February 19

God's Word	*When pride comes, then comes disgrace, but with humility comes wisdom. (Proverbs 11:2, NIV)*
Life Principle	Because you are made in God's image, it is a disgrace to deny God His rightful place as LORD of your life.
Life changes	_____ _____ _____ _____ _____ _____ _____ ⇨ ∞ 🗨 📢 ⌂ ⊕ 🎯

February 20

God's Word	*The integrity of the upright guides them, but the unfaithful are destroyed by their duplicity.* *(Proverbs 11:3, NIV)*
Life Principle	Truth is an expressway to wise living while double-dealing is a dead-end road.
Life changes	

February 21

God's Word	*Wealth is worthless in the day of wrath, but righteousness delivers from death. (Proverbs 11:4, NIV)*
Life Principle	"You can't take it with you when you go" - and why would you want to? God uses gold to pave the streets in Heaven. Wealth cannot buy a righteous standing.
Life changes	_____ _____ _____ _____ _____ _____ _____ ⇨ ∞ 💭 📢 ⛏ ⊕ 🎯

February 22

God's Word	The righteousness of the blameless makes a straight way for them, but the wicked are brought down by their own wickedness. (Proverbs 11:5, NIV)
Life Principle	Righteous living gives you simplicity over confusion, certainty over fear, and hope over calamity.
Life changes	

February 23

God's Word	*When a wicked man dies, his hope perishes; all he expected from his power comes to nothing. (Proverbs 11:7, NIV)*
Life Principle	Pity the man who trusts in his own strength, power, and influence. For when he dies, he will have nothing. If you live without Christ, you will die without Christ.
Life changes	_____ _____ _____ _____ _____ _____ _____

February 24

God's Word	*With his mouth the godless destroys his neighbor, but through knowledge the righteous escape. (Proverbs 11:9, NIV)*
Life Principle	A word spoken can bring destruction and a word heeded can bring salvation. Have you heeded the word of the LORD?
Life changes	

February 25

God's Word	*Through the blessing of the upright a city is exalted, but by the mouth of the wicked it is destroyed.* *(Proverbs 11:11, NIV)*
Life Principle	Out of the same mouth you can speak words of blessing or cursing. One brings commendation, the other brings condemnation – which will you choose?
Life changes	_____ _____ _____ _____ _____ _____ _____

February 26

God's Word	A man who lacks judgment derides his neighbor, but a man of understanding holds his tongue. (Proverbs 11:12, NIV)
Life Principle	Gossip destroys people and communities. If it is not true, do not say it. If it is true, use discretion. If it does not need to be said, then do not say it.
Life changes	

February 27

God's Word	*For lack of guidance a nation falls, but many advisers make victory sure. (Proverbs 11:14, NIV)*
Life Principle	It pays to get a 2nd opinion … and a 3rd, and a 4th. As you get more advice, you get more perspectives on an issue so that you can make a better decision.
Life changes	_____ _____ _____ _____ _____ _____ _____

February 28

God's Word	*For lack of guidance a nation falls, but many advisers make victory sure.* *(Proverbs 11:14, NIV)*
Life Principle	The proud man refuses to even seek advice. A nation of such fools will surely fall.
Life changes	

February 29

God's Word	*A kindhearted woman gains respect, but ruthless men gain only wealth.* *(Proverbs 11:16, NIV)*
Life Principle	Respect is not acquired; it is conferred.
Life changes	_____ _____ _____ _____ _____ _____ _____

March

> The proverbs of Solomon
> son of David, king of Israel: ...
> for understanding words of insight.
> (Proverbs 1:1-2, NIV)

Symbol	Life Change
⇨	A command to follow
∞	A principle to use
💭	Thoughts to engage and attitudes to avoid
📢	What you say and how you say it
🔨	A good work to start
✦	A sin to confess and forsake
🎯	Thanksgiving for God's hand at work in your life

March 1

God's Word	*A kind man benefits himself, But a cruel man brings trouble on himself. (Proverbs 11:17, NIV)*
Life Principle	If you give away money, you may gain friends. But when the money runs out, so do the friends. Give away kindness and you will gain respect that lasts.
Life changes	_____ _____ _____ _____ _____ _____ _____ ⇨ ∞ 💭 📢 🛠 ⊕ 🎯

March 2

God's Word	*The wicked man earns deceptive wages, but he who sows righteousness reaps a sure reward.* *(Proverbs 11:18, NIV)*
Life Principle	Seeking God's will as your first priority is like planting a "blessing seed" that is guaranteed to bear good fruit.
Life changes	_____ _____ _____ _____ _____ _____ _____

March 3

God's Word	Be sure of this: the wicked will not go unpunished, But those who are righteous will go free. (Proverbs 11:21, NIV)
Life Principle	In the end, God wins. All wrongs will be made right. The question now is: are you with Him or against Him?
Life changes	_____ _____ _____ _____ _____ _____ _____ _____

March 4

God's Word	*A generous man will prosper; he who refreshes others will himself be refreshed.* *(Proverbs 11:25, NIV)*
Life Principle	In God's economy, generosity pays a certain dividend: God's blessing. We tend to think of material things – but who knows in what greater way God will bless you?
Life changes	_____ _____ _____ _____ _____ _____ _____

March 5

God's Word	*He who seeks good finds goodwill, but evil comes to him who searches for it. (Proverbs 11:27, NIV)*
Life Principle	It is such an obvious principle that if you do what is good and right for others you will generally find good will in return. Or you can pick a fight and get ... ?
Life changes	_____ _____ _____ _____ _____ _____ _____ _____

March 6

God's Word	*He who brings trouble on his family will inherit only wind. (Proverbs 11:29, NIV)*
Life Principle	Ignoring your family will compromise your relationships. Soon the people will disappear as well. Then your home will only whisper like the wind.
Life changes	_____ _____ _____ _____ _____ _____ _____

March 7

God's Word	The fruit of the righteous is a tree of life, and he who wins souls is wise. (Proverbs 11:30, NIV)
Life Principle	When you lead someone to Jesus, they are blessed and tell others. When these come to Jesus, they also tell others. Your witness is seed that continues to bear fruit.
Life changes	_____ _____ _____ _____ _____ _____ _____

March 8

God's Word	*If the righteous receive their due on earth, how much more the ungodly and the sinner! (Proverbs 11:31, NIV)*
Life Principle	Do not let the happy face fool you. A rebellious person hurts inside as much as the righteous - even more so since this person has no fellowship with His Creator.
Life changes	_____ _____ _____ _____ _____ _____ _____ ⇨ ∞ 🗩 ◁ 🔨 ⊕ 🎯

March 9

God's Word	*Whoever loves discipline loves knowledge but he who hates correction is stupid. (Proverbs 12:1, NIV)*
Life Principle	Learn to appreciate times of correction. A teachable spirit will serve you well no matter what you do in life.
Life changes	_____ _____ _____ _____ _____ _____ _____ ⇨ ∞ 🗨 📢 ⛏ ⊕ 🛞

March 10

God's Word	*A good man obtains favor from the LORD, but the LORD condemns a crafty man.* *(Proverbs 12:2, NIV)*
Life Principle	If you truly desire to do what is right in God's sight, God will look on this with favor. Who would not want to be on God's "favor" list?
Life changes	_____ _____ _____ _____ _____ _____ _____

March 11

God's Word	*A man cannot be established through wickedness, but the righteous cannot be uprooted. (Proverbs 12:3, NIV)*
Life Principle	You cannot build yourself up by tearing others down. You cannot cheat your way to success. You can establish a strong foundation for life by following Christ.
Life changes	_____ _____ _____ _____ _____ _____ _____ _____

March 12

God's Word	*A wife of noble character is her husband's crown, but a disgraceful wife is like decay in his bones. (Proverbs 12:4, NIV)*
Life Principle	Who says women are not strong? A good wife can lift up her husband to the heights of Heaven.
Life changes	_____ _____ _____ _____ _____ _____ _____ _____ ⇨ ∞ 🗭 📢 🖐 ⊕ 🎯

March 13

God's Word	*The plans of the righteous are just, but the advice of the wicked is deceitful. (Proverbs 12:5, NIV)*
Life Principle	Do your plans bring pleasure to God? Do they work toward His goals? Righteous plans include our righteous God in the planning.
Life changes	_____ _____ _____ _____ _____ _____ _____

March 14

God's Word	*The words of the wicked lie in wait for blood, but the speech of the upright rescues them. (Proverbs 12:6, NIV)*
Life Principle	What are the words that turn a wicked man into an upright man? One word to the LORD Jesus – "Mercy!"
Life changes	_____ _____ _____ _____ _____ _____ _____ ⇨ ∞ 💭 📣 🙌 ⊕ 🎯

March 15

God's Word	*Wicked men are overthrown and are no more, but the house of the righteous stands firm. (Proverbs 12:7, NIV)*
Life Principle	The one who shakes his fist at God is no more secure than a mobile home in the path of a tornado – judgment day is unavoidable.
Life changes	_____ _____ _____ _____ _____ _____ _____ _____ ⇨ ∞ 💭 📢 ☝ ⊕ 🛞

March 16

God's Word	*A man is praised according to his wisdom, but men with warped minds are despised. (Proverbs 12:8, NIV)*
Life Principle	The only wisdom that will bring you praise comes from the word of God firmly planted and taking root in your mind.
Life changes	_____ _____ _____ _____ _____ _____ _____ ⇨ ∞ 🗩 📢 ☝ ⊕ 🎯

March 17

God's Word	*Better to be a nobody and yet have a servant than pretend to be somebody and have no food.* *(Proverbs 12:9, NIV)*
Life Principle	Nobody can be you but you. If you pretend to be someone else, where will you be?
Life changes	_____ _____ _____ _____ _____ _____ _____ _____

March 18

God's Word	*A righteous man cares for the needs of his animal, but the kindest acts of the wicked are cruel.* *(Proverbs 12:10, NIV)*
Life Principle	Be kind even to the least and the lowly. Kindness is a natural result of righteousness in your heart.
Life changes	_____ _____ _____ _____ _____ _____ _____

March 19

God's Word	*He who works his land will have abundant food, but he who chases fantasies lacks judgment.* *(Proverbs 12:11, NIV)*
Life Principle	God makes His provision for you in the real world not the dream world.
Life changes	_____ _____ _____ _____ _____ _____ _____ ⇨ ∞ 💭 📣 🏺 ⊕ 🎯

March 20

God's Word	*The wicked desire the plunder of evil men, but the fruit of the righteous flourishes. (Proverbs 12:12, NIV)*
Life Principle	You may not see the fruit of your life right now. But keep yourself firmly planted on the rock of Jesus Christ and you will bear fruit. It is inevitable.
Life changes	_____ _____ _____ _____ _____ _____ _____

March 21

God's Word	*An evil man is trapped by his sinful talk, but a righteous man escapes trouble. (Proverbs 12:13, NIV)*
Life Principle	You cannot escape from the words that escape from your own lips.
Life changes	_____ _____ _____ _____ _____ _____ _____ ⇨ ∞ 💭 ◁ 🖐 ⊕ 🎯

March 22

God's Word	*From the fruit of his lips a man is filled with good things as surely as the work of his hands rewards him. (Proverbs 12:14, NIV)*
Life Principle	Hard work and healing words – both bring a certain profit.
Life changes	_____ _____ _____ _____ _____ _____ _____ ⇨ ∞ 💭 📢 ⮬ ⊕ 🎯

March 23

God's Word	*The way of a fool seems right to him, but a wise man listens to advice.* *(Proverbs 12:15, NIV)*
Life Principle	Young people and old should take note of advice given by godly friends and family. Listen with both ears.
Life changes	_____ _____ _____ _____ _____ _____ _____ _____

March 24

God's Word	*A fool shows his annoyance at once, but a prudent man overlooks an insult. (Proverbs 12:16, NIV)*
Life Principle	When criticized – stop! Consider what is said in light of God's word. If there is any truth, correct yourself first. Then you can respond appropriately.
Life changes	_____ _____ _____ _____ _____ _____ _____ _____

March 25

God's Word	*A truthful witness gives honest testimony, but a false witness tells lies.* *(Proverbs 12:17, NIV)*
Life Principle	Be honest. Then be consistent ... because consistency reinforces the will to be honest.
Life changes	_____ _____ _____ _____ _____ _____ _____ ⇨ ∞ 💭 📢 ⛊ ⊕ 🎯

March 26

God's Word	*Reckless words pierce like a sword, but the tongue of the wise brings healing. (Proverbs 12:18, NIV)*
Life Principle	Words are finely honed daggers that pierce the soul. So be sure your words are filled with grace, wisdom, and encouragement.
Life changes	_____ _____ _____ _____ _____ _____ _____

March 27

God's Word	*Truthful lips endure forever, But a lying tongue lasts only a moment. (Proverbs 12:19, NIV)*
Life Principle	No one cares to remember the deceit of a liar. Yet an honest person will leave a legacy of respect.
Life changes	_____ _____ _____ _____ _____ _____ _____ _____ ⇨ ∞ 💭 📢 👍 ⊕ 🎯

March 28

God's Word	*There is deceit in the hearts of those who plot evil, but joy for those who promote peace. (Proverbs 12:20, NIV)*
Life Principle	Promoting peace on the outside promotes joy on your inside.
Life changes	_____ _____ _____ _____ _____ _____ _____

March 29

God's Word	*No harm befalls the righteous, But the wicked have their fill of trouble. (Proverbs 12:21, NIV)*
Life Principle	Nothing touches the life of a believer without first passing through the filter of God's love. The unbeliever, however, is exposed to the full fury of a fallen world.
Life changes	_____ _____ _____ _____ _____ _____ _____

March 30

God's Word	*The LORD detests lying lips, But He delights in men who are truthful.* *(Proverbs 12:22, NIV)*
Life Principle	The heart of God is truth. Should it be a surprise that His favor rests on honest people?
Life changes	_____ _____ _____ _____ _____ _____ _____ _____

March 31

God's Word	A prudent man keeps his knowledge to himself, but the heart of fools blurts out folly. (Proverbs 12:23, NIV)
Life Principle	You do not have to tell everything to everyone. Honesty does not require that you embarrass yourself and others with unnecessary information.
Life changes	_____ _____ _____ _____ _____ _____ _____

April

The proverbs of Solomon
son of David, king of Israel: ...
for acquiring a disciplined life...
(Proverbs 1:1,3, NIV)

Symbol	Life Change
⇨	A command to follow
∞	A principle to use
💭	Thoughts to engage and attitudes to avoid
📢	What you say and how you say it
⚒	A good work to start
✦	A sin to confess and forsake
🎯	Thanksgiving for God's hand at work in your life

April 1

God's Word	Diligent hands will rule, But laziness ends in slave labor. (Proverbs 12:24, NIV)
Life Principle	The lazy person thinks he is free but soon sees the prison bars of debt and servitude. If you will not work, you shall not eat.
Life changes	_____ _____ _____ _____ _____ _____ _____ _____

April 2

God's Word	*An anxious heart weighs a man down, but a kind word cheers him up.* *(Proverbs 12:25, NIV)*
Life Principle	Anxiety is concern over situations you can neither change nor control. It is a burden God knows you cannot carry. Let Him!
Life changes	_____ _____ _____ _____ _____ _____ _____ ⇨ ∞ 💭 📢 🤲 ⊕ 🎯

April 3

God's Word	A righteous man is cautious in friendship, but the way of the wicked leads them astray. (Proverbs 12:26, NIV)
Life Principle	Lead your friends to Christ to avoid them leading both of you astray.
Life changes	_____ _____ _____ _____ _____ _____ _____ _____

April 4

God's Word	*In the way of righteousness there is life; along that path is immortality.* *(Proverbs 12:28, NIV)*
Life Principle	Satisfaction in this life can only be attained by following Christ. Yet this is the same path to eternal life.
Life changes	_____ _____ _____ _____ _____ _____ _____ _____

April 5

God's Word	*A wise son heeds his father's instruction, but a mocker does not listen to rebuke. (Proverbs 13:1, NIV)*
Life Principle	Listen to wise words - even if they sting - to avoid becoming a pretentious rebel.
Life changes	

April 6

God's Word	*From the fruit of his lips a man enjoys good things, but the unfaithful have a craving for violence.* *(Proverbs 13:2, NIV)*
Life Principle	Words are the fruit of your life-experiences. Harvest the power of words that inspire, encourage, heal, help, persuade, and move to action.
Life changes	_____ _____ _____ _____ _____ _____ _____ _____

April 7

God's Word	*He who guards his lips guards his life, but he who speaks rashly will come to ruin.* *(Proverbs 13:3, NIV)*
Life Principle	Even a single word can destroy your reputation. Guard your life by thinking before speaking.
Life changes	_____ _____ _____ _____ _____ _____ _____

April 8

God's Word	*The sluggard craves and gets nothing, but the desires of the diligent are fully satisfied.* *(Proverbs 13:4, NIV)*
Life Principle	Wanting does nothing and results in nothing. Diligence will get things done.
Life changes	

April 9

God's Word	*The righteous hate what is false, but the wicked bring shame and disgrace. (Proverbs 13:5, NIV)*
Life Principle	Hate is a very strong word. In the context of a righteous person, it indicates a high priority. Love the truth. Get real. Stop pretending.
Life changes	_____ _____ _____ _____ _____ _____ _____ ⇨ ∞ 💭 📢 👆 ⊕ 🎯

April 10

God's Word	A man's riches may ransom his life, but a poor man hears no threat. *(Proverbs 13:8, NIV)*
Life Principle	One who holds everything has everything to lose. Travel light – you will sleep better.
Life changes	_____ _____ _____ _____ _____ _____ _____ ⇨ ∞ 💭 📢 ☝ ⊕ 🎯

April 11

God's Word	*Pride only breeds quarrels, but wisdom is found in those who take advice. (Proverbs 13:10, NIV)*
Life Principle	No matter how smart you may think you are, there are always other smarter people. Keep your mind open to good instruction.
Life changes	_____ _____ _____ _____ _____ _____ _____ ⇨ ∞ 💭 ◁ 👆 ⊕ 🎯

April 12

God's Word	*Dishonest money dwindles away, but he who gathers money little by little makes it grow. (Proverbs 13:11, NIV)*
Life Principle	Diligence with discipline yields great results.
Life changes	_____ _____ _____ _____ _____ _____ _____ _____

April 13

God's Word	*Hope deferred makes the heart sick, but a longing fulfilled is a tree of life. (Proverbs 13:12, NIV)*
Life Principle	Our deepest longing is to know our Creator and His purpose for our lives. God longs to have a relationship with you. Seek your fulfillment and hope in Him.
Life changes	_____ _____ _____ _____ _____ _____ _____ _____

April 14

God's Word	He who scorns instruction will pay for it, but he who respects a command is rewarded. (Proverbs 13:13, NIV)
Life Principle	Authority is not to be resisted but accepted. Every group – government, business, church, - has to have clear lines of authority to operate effectively.
Life changes	_____ _____ _____ _____ _____ _____ _____

April 15

God's Word	Every prudent man acts out of knowledge, but a fool exposes his folly. (Proverbs 13:16, NIV)
Life Principle	Do you react quickly and forcefully to anything that does not go your way? Don't be a fool - check the facts before you act.
Life changes	_____ _____ _____ _____ _____ _____ _____

April 16

God's Word	*He who walks with the wise grows wise, but a companion of fools suffers harm. (Proverbs 13:20, NIV)*
Life Principle	Your friends matter. A smart person looks for people of good character and hangs with them. Losers look for the popular, beautiful, and strong.
Life changes	

April 17

God's Word	*Misfortune pursues the sinner, but prosperity is the reward of the righteous. (Proverbs 13:21, NIV)*
Life Principle	Just because God seems to delay justice does not mean that He is unaware or uncaring. God is loving and just. He will act in His time.
Life changes	_____ _____ _____ _____ _____ _____ _____ ⇨ ∞ 💭 ◁ 🔼 ⊕ 🎯

April 18

God's Word	A good man leaves an inheritance for his children's children. (Proverbs 13:22, NIV)
Life Principle	It is unlikely you can earn enough money to last two generations. But far, far better than wealth - you can leave a legacy of faith, hope, and love.
Life changes	_____ _____ _____ _____ _____ _____ _____ _____

April 19

God's Word	*A poor man's field may produce abundant food, but injustice sweeps it away. (Proverbs 13:23, NIV)*
Life Principle	Some people are poor through no fault of their own. Remember those less fortunate than you.
Life changes	_____ _____ _____ _____ _____ _____ _____ ⇨ ∞ 💭 ◁ ⌂ ⊕ 🎯

April 20

God's Word	*He who spares the rod hates his son, but he who loves him is careful to discipline him. (Proverbs 13:24, NIV)*
Life Principle	The rod is a symbol of correction not punishment. Discipline is unique for each child. If spanking is needed, take care not to beat your child into rebellion.
Life changes	_____ _____ _____ _____ _____ _____ _____ _____

April 21

God's Word	The righteous eat to their hearts' content, but the stomach of the wicked goes hungry. (Proverbs 13:25, NIV)
Life Principle	Are you content when you are full or when you are stuffed? Gluttony is as sinful as drunkenness. The point is that God will not let the righteous go hungry.
Life changes	_____ _____ _____ _____ _____ _____ _____ _____

April 22

God's Word	*The wise woman builds her house, but with her own hands the foolish one tears hers down.* *(Proverbs 14:1, NIV)*
Life Principle	It takes work to build up a family. The natural course is anarchy. Who has not been impacted in profound ways by one's mother?
Life changes	_____ _____ _____ _____ _____ _____ _____ _____

April 23

God's Word	*He whose walk is upright fears the LORD, but he whose ways are devious despises him.* *(Proverbs 14:2, NIV)*
Life Principle	Do you consider yourself to be a generally good person? If you truly are good then you will love the LORD and follow His path. You cannot have one without the other.
Life changes	_____ _____ _____ _____ _____ _____ _____ ⇨ ∞ 🗩 📣 ⛫ ⊕ 🎯

April 24

God's Word	*A fool's talk brings a rod to his back, but the lips of the wise protect them. (Proverbs 14:3, NIV)*
Life Principle	Tell the truth. You are totally secure when you do not have to remember a lie.
Life changes	_____ _____ _____ _____ _____ _____ _____ ⇨ ∞ 💭 📢 ☝ ⊕ 🎯

April 25

God's Word	*Where there are no oxen, the manger is empty, but from the strength of an ox comes an abundant harvest. (Proverbs 14:4, NIV)*
Life Principle	The good news is that an empty stable needs no cleaning. The bad news is that it brings no profit. You must invest and work hard to bring home a profit.
Life changes	_____ _____ _____ _____ _____ _____ _____ _____

April 26

God's Word	*A truthful witness does not deceive, but a false witness pours out lies. (Proverbs 14:5, NIV)*
Life Principle	Be careful not to judge someone based on accusations alone. Trust what you *know* about someone until you *know* different.
Life changes	_____ _____ _____ _____ _____ _____ _____ _____

April 27

God's Word	Stay away from a foolish man, for you will not find knowledge on his lips. (Proverbs 14:7, NIV)
Life Principle	It would be impossible to avoid all foolish people in this world. But do not waste your time trying to understand or sympathize with them.
Life changes	_____ _____ _____ _____ _____ _____ _____

April 28

God's Word	*The wisdom of the prudent is to give thought to their ways, but the folly of fools is deception.* *(Proverbs 14:8, NIV)*
Life Principle	Determine *why* you are doing *what* you are doing. Only a fool hides his true intentions from himself.
Life changes	_____ _____ _____ _____ _____ _____ _____ _____ ⇨ ∞ 💭 📢 👆 ⊕ 🎯

April 29

God's Word	*Each heart knows its own bitterness, and no one else can share its joy. (Proverbs 14:10, NIV)*
Life Principle	Be sure to give people the benefit of the doubt. You can never know the full impact of life events they have endured.
Life changes	_____ _____ _____ _____ _____ _____ _____

April 30

God's Word	*The house of the wicked will be destroyed, but the tent of the upright will flourish. (Proverbs 14:11, NIV)*
Life Principle	A righteous God will enact justice in the end. You may not see the wicked destroyed in your lifetime. But they will face a holy God without any defense at all.
Life changes	_____ _____ _____ _____ _____ _____ _____ ⇨ ∞ 💭 📢 ☝ ⊕ 🎯

May

The proverbs of Solomon
son of David, king of Israel: ...
for acquiring a ... prudent life...
(Proverbs 1:1,3, NIV)

Symbol	Life Change
⇨	A command to follow
∞	A principle to use
💭	Thoughts to engage and attitudes to avoid
📢	What you say and how you say it
⚒	A good work to start
✛	A sin to confess and forsake
🎯	Thanksgiving for God's hand at work in your life

May 1

God's Word	*There is a way that seems right to a man, but in the end it leads to death. (Proverbs 14:12, NIV)*
Life Principle	Justify whatever you want, any way you can. Anything goes ... until you deal with the One who holds your life and your death in the balance.
Life changes	_____ _____ _____ _____ _____ _____ _____

May 2

God's Word	*Even in laughter the heart may ache, and joy may end in grief.* *(Proverbs 14:13, NIV)*
Life Principle	Human emotions are a complex mystery. They can easily overwhelm you. Put your mind in gear as you act on faith not feelings.
Life changes	_____ _____ _____ _____ _____ _____ _____ _____ ⇨ ∞ 💭 📣 ☝ ⊕ 🎯

May 3

God's Word	The faithless will be fully repaid for their ways, and the good man rewarded for his. (Proverbs 14:14, NIV)
Life Principle	No one gets away with anything. And no good deed will be overlooked by the Almighty. It is not a question of "If" but "When?"
Life changes	_____ _____ _____ _____ _____ _____ _____

May 4

God's Word	*A simple man believes anything, but a prudent man gives thought to his steps. (Proverbs 14:15, NIV)*
Life Principle	Just because you hear it on the news or read it in a book does not mean it is true. Make sure you get and consider carefully the facts.
Life changes	_____ _____ _____ _____ _____ _____ _____ _____

May 5

God's Word	*...A fool is hotheaded and reckless. A quick-tempered man does foolish things, and a crafty man is hated. (Proverbs 14:16b-17, NIV)*
Life Principle	Acting rashly rarely allows you to make good decisions. Think about the long-term impact before you act.
Life changes	

May 6

God's Word	*Evil men will bow down in the presence of the good, and the wicked at the gates of the righteous. (Proverbs 14:19, NIV)*
Life Principle	Bad things happen to innocent people in this life. That is reality. But God will one-day enact justice and right every wrong. That is also reality.
Life changes	_____ _____ _____ _____ _____ _____ _____ _____

May 7

God's Word	*The poor are shunned even by their neighbors, but the rich have many friends. (Proverbs 14:20, NIV)*
Life Principle	Do you give preference to people because of money? What a poor way to make friends! When the money runs out, so do the friends.
Life changes	_____ _____ _____ _____ _____ _____ _____

May 8

God's Word	*He who despises his neighbor sins, but blessed is he who is kind to the needy.* *(Proverbs 14:21, NIV)*
Life Principle	When someone you know is in need, and you have the resources to help them – then help them. It is a sin to refuse to help when it is within your power to do so.
Life changes	_____ _____ _____ _____ _____ _____ _____ ⇨ ∞ 🗩 ◁ ⌂ ⊕ 🎯

May 9

God's Word	*All hard work brings a profit, but mere talk leads only to poverty. (Proverbs 14:23, NIV)*
Life Principle	The big man on campus is usually the one with the big mouth. Talk is cheap. Actions speak louder than words. And all hard work brings it own rewards.
Life changes	

May 10

God's Word	*A truthful witness saves lives, but a false witness is deceitful.* *(Proverbs 14:25, NIV)*
Life Principle	What a different judicial system it would be if a false witness was given the sentence intended for the accused! Honesty is crucial for just justice.
Life changes	_____ _____ _____ _____ _____ _____ _____ ⇨ ∞ 💭 ◁ 👐 ⊕ 🎯

May 11

God's Word	*He who fears the LORD has a secure fortress, and for his children it will be a refuge. (Proverbs 14:26, NIV)*
Life Principle	Is there a friend you can go to and be totally honest and totally secure? Trust in the LORD Jesus and you have One that no one on Earth can corrupt or overpower.
Life changes	_____ _____ _____ _____ _____ _____ _____

May 12

God's Word	*The fear of the LORD is a fountain of life, turning a man from the snares of death.* *(Proverbs 14:27, NIV)*
Life Principle	Is there anything you can do to find a life worth living? Trust in the LORD Jesus. He gives you meaning, purpose, and love to keep you from despair and a wasted life.
Life changes	_____ _____ _____ _____ _____ _____ _____

May 13

God's Word	*A patient man has great understanding, but a quick-tempered man displays folly. (Proverbs 14:29, NIV)*
Life Principle	"Ready, Fire, Aim!" What is wrong with this approach? You need to be patient – with yourself and with other people. A quick temper results in disaster.
Life changes	_____ _____ _____ _____ _____ _____ _____

May 14

God's Word	*He who oppresses the poor shows contempt for their Maker, but whoever is kind to the needy honors God. (Proverbs 14:31, NIV)*
Life Principle	If you put down those who are less fortunate than you, you reveal your hatred for God. He is the Maker of both the poor and rich.
Life changes	

May 15

God's Word	*Righteousness exalts a nation, but sin is a disgrace to any people.* *(Proverbs 14:34, NIV)*
Life Principle	Morality matters – in your own life, your family, and your community. Doing what is right and just is not a quaint philosophy but impacts an entire nation.
Life changes	_____ _____ _____ _____ _____ _____ _____ _____

May 16

God's Word	*A gentle answer turns away wrath, but a harsh word stirs up anger. (Proverbs 15:1, NIV)*
Life Principle	Answer softly – you cannot beat up a sponge. But rocks hurt – you can fight pretty mean with rocks.
Life changes	_____ _____ _____ _____ _____ _____ _____ _____ ⇨ ∞ 💭 📣 ⛄ ⊕ 🎯

May 17

God's Word	*The tongue of the wise commends knowledge, but the mouth of the fool gushes folly.* *(Proverbs 15:2, NIV)*
Life Principle	You can be a know-it-all and act like it – but people will not listen to you. Strive to learn all you can but share it in a way that people can accept.
Life changes	_____ _____ _____ _____ _____ _____ _____

May 18

God's Word	The eyes of the LORD are everywhere, keeping watch on the wicked and the good. (Proverbs 15:3, NIV)
Life Principle	"He knows if you've been bad or good" is not a Santa Claus thing – it is a God thing. And the stakes are not toys but eternity.
Life changes	_____ _____ _____ _____ _____ _____ _____ _____ ⇨ ∞ 💭 📢 ⏏ ⊕ 🎯

May 19

God's Word	*The tongue that brings healing is a tree of life, but a deceitful tongue crushes the spirit. (Proverbs 15:4, NIV)*
Life Principle	Your words can lift another person's spirit to the heights of Heaven itself. Be an encourager, a trusted confidante, and a giver of hope to all you encounter.
Life changes	_____ _____ _____ _____ _____ _____ _____

May 20

God's Word	*The lips of the wise spread knowledge; not so the hearts of fools. (Proverbs 15:7, NIV)*
Life Principle	Wisdom should be shared not sequestered. It will not make you any less wise.
Life changes	_____ _____ _____ _____ _____ _____ _____ _____

May 21

God's Word	*The LORD detests the sacrifice of the wicked, but the prayer of the upright pleases him.* *(Proverbs 15:8, NIV)*
Life Principle	Nothing pleases our Heavenly Father more than hearing from one of His children. Share your life with Him openly and frequently.
Life changes	_____ _____ _____ _____ _____ _____ _____ _____

May 22

God's Word	*Stern discipline awaits him who leaves the path; he who hates correction will die. (Proverbs 15:10, NIV)*
Life Principle	God loves you too much to let you wander into danger. While His discipline is hard, and may seem severe at times, it serves to help you live and grow stronger.
Life changes	_____ _____ _____ _____ _____ _____ _____ _____

May 23

God's Word	*A happy heart makes the face cheerful, but heartache crushes the spirit.* *(Proverbs 15:13, NIV)*
Life Principle	Your face is a window to your soul. When you are right with God and your loved ones, a happy heart cannot be hidden.
Life changes	_____ _____ _____ _____ _____ _____ _____

May 24

God's Word	*Better a little with the fear of the LORD than great wealth with turmoil.* *(Proverbs 15:16, NIV)*
Life Principle	If you have it all, you have strife and heartache to go with it. If you have the LORD, you have everything you need … and more.
Life changes	_____ _____ _____ _____ _____ _____ _____ _____

May 25

God's Word	*A hot-tempered man stirs up dissension, but a patient man calms a quarrel.* *(Proverbs 15:18, NIV)*
Life Principle	Your anger, unchecked, generates more hostility in others. No home or workplace can survive one who will not restrain his anger.
Life changes	_____ _____ _____ _____ _____ _____ _____ _____

May 26

God's Word	*A wise son brings joy to his father, but a foolish man despises his mother. (Proverbs 15:20, NIV)*
Life Principle	A wise child loves both parents. No greater joy can parents find than a child that shows them love. How much more true for our Heavenly Father!
Life changes	_____ _____ _____ _____ _____ _____ _____ _____

May 27

God's Word	*Plans fail for lack of counsel, but with many advisers they succeed.* *(Proverbs15;22, NIV)*
Life Principle	A good plan is never refined by those who agree with your approach. Listen to all sides to test the potential for success.
Life changes	_____ _____ _____ _____ _____ _____ _____ _____

May 28

God's Word	*The path of life leads upward for the wise to keep him from going down to the grave. (Proverbs 15:24, NIV)*
Life Principle	Hope, hope, hope – live in hope! Hope points you upward, makes your steps lively, and keeps you from slowing down or turning aside.
Life changes	_____ _____ _____ _____ _____ _____ _____ _____ ⇨ ∞ 💭 📢 ⛏ ⊕ 🎯

May 29

God's Word	*The LORD detests the thoughts of the wicked, but those of the pure are pleasing to him.* *(Proverbs 15:26, NIV)*
Life Principle	Think about it – the LORD even thinks about your thoughts. Will He be pleased with the purity or repulsed by the rottenness?
Life changes	_____ _____ _____ _____ _____ _____ _____ _____

May 30

God's Word	*A greedy man brings trouble to his family, but he who hates bribes will live. (Proverbs 15:27, NIV)*
Life Principle	Your family is the greatest treasure you could ever find or possess. Why seek anything less?
Life changes	_____ _____ _____ _____ _____ _____ _____ ⇨ ∞ 💭 ◁ ⛄ ⊕ 🎯

May 31

God's Word	*The heart of the righteous weighs its answers, but the mouth of the wicked gushes evil.* *(Proverbs 15:28, NIV)*
Life Principle	Your lips, by themselves, are incapable of good judgment. Before you answer, give yourself time to hear the question and ponder its implications.
Life changes	_____ _____ _____ _____ _____ _____ _____

June

> The proverbs of Solomon
> son of David, king of Israel: ... for
> doing what is right and just and fair ...
> (Proverbs 1:1,3, NIV)

Symbol	Life Change
	A command to follow
	A principle to use
	Thoughts to engage and attitudes to avoid
	What you say and how you say it
	A good work to start
	A sin to confess and forsake
	Thanksgiving for God's hand at work in your life

June 1

God's Word	*The LORD is far from the wicked but he hears the prayer of the righteous. (Proverbs 15:29, NIV)*
Life Principle	Running away from God muffles your request. You need to be within hearing distance. Keep things right between you and God.
Life changes	_____ _____ _____ _____ _____ _____ _____ ⇨ ∞ 💭 📣 🔥 ⊕ 🎯

June 2

God's Word	*A cheerful look brings joy to the heart, and good news gives health to the bones. (Proverbs 15:30 , NIV)*
Life Principle	Encouragement is a breath of fresh air or a cool summer rain. Nothing refreshes your attitude and strength like a good word from a friend.
Life changes	_____ _____ _____ _____ _____ _____ _____ _____ ⇨ ∞ 💭 ◁ 🔼 ⊕ 🎯

June 3

God's Word	*The fear of the LORD teaches a man wisdom, and humility comes before honor. (Proverbs 15:33, NIV)*
Life Principle	If you want people to think well of you, you had better make sure the LORD is one of them – the main one. A person of honor first bows before Almighty God.
Life changes	_____ _____ _____ _____ _____ _____ _____ ⇨ ∞ 💭 📢 ⛝ ⊕ 🎯

June 4

God's Word	*To man belong the plans of the heart, but from the LORD comes the reply of the tongue.* *(Proverbs 16:1, NIV)*
Life Principle	Some say, "Just follow your heart." But the heart is just another word for feelings that often deceive you. Make your plans but get the LORD's approval.
Life changes	_____ _____ _____ _____ _____ _____ _____ _____

June 5

God's Word	*All a man's ways seem innocent to him, but motives are weighed by the LORD. (Proverbs 16:2, NIV)*
Life Principle	You can do the right thing for all the wrong reasons. And be aware that you rarely judge fairly. Ask the LORD to weigh in on the *why* behind your *what*.
Life changes	_____ _____ _____ _____ _____ _____ _____ _____ ⇨ ∞ 💭 📢 🔥 ⊕ 🎯

June 6

God's Word	*Commit to the LORD whatever you do, and your plans will succeed. (Proverbs 16:3, NIV)*
Life Principle	Ensure that your plans and motivation are in accord with God's will. Then commit yourself fully to the task. God's work done God's way will succeed.
Life changes	_____ _____ _____ _____ _____ _____ _____

June 7

God's Word	*Through love and faithfulness sin is atoned for; through the fear of the LORD a man avoids evil. (Proverbs 16:6, NIV)*
Life Principle	You cannot erase your sins by trying to be good. But you can make things good for yourself and others.
Life changes	_____ _____ _____ _____ _____ _____ _____

June 8

God's Word	*Better a little with righteousness than much gain with injustice. (Proverbs 16:8, NIV)*
Life Principle	If you are climbing higher by trampling over others, you will not have the LORD's favor. Your success will be fleeting and, ultimately, unsatisfying.
Life changes	_____ _____ _____ _____ _____ _____ _____ _____

June 9

God's Word	*Honest scales and balances belong to the LORD; all the weights in the bag are of his making. (Proverbs 16:11, NIV)*
Life Principle	An objective look at a situation is necessary to make a wise decision. Only the LORD can give you the brutally honest truth you need.
Life changes	

June 10

God's Word	*Kings detest wrongdoing, for a throne is established through righteousness. (Proverbs 16:12, NIV)*
Life Principle	A kingdom cannot endure without the rule of righteousness. Neither can a family nor a marriage endure. Hate wrongdoing and cling to what is right.
Life changes	_____ _____ _____ _____ _____ _____ _____ _____

June 11

God's Word	*Kings take pleasure in honest lips; they value the one who speaks what is right.* *(Proverbs 16:13, NIV)*
Life Principle	Are you sometimes afraid to speak up because you are not sure if it is what your boss wants to hear? Speak the truth – that is what your boss both needs and wants.
Life changes	_____ _____ _____ _____ _____ _____ _____ _____

June 12

God's Word	*How much better to get wisdom than gold, to get insight rather than silver! (Proverbs 16:16, NIV)*
Life Principle	Money is important, to be sure. But what you long for, work for, and hope for should be the wisdom of God. His insights are priceless.
Life changes	_____ _____ _____ _____ _____ _____ _____ _____

June 13

God's Word	*Pride goes before destruction, a haughty spirit before a fall.* *(Proverbs 16:18, NIV)*
Life Principle	Pride takes many forms but has the same substance. It is a cancer that destroys you from the inside-out. Kill the arrogance before it kills you.
Life changes	_____ _____ _____ _____ _____ _____ _____ _____

June 14

God's Word	*Blessed is the one who trusts in the LORD. (Proverbs 16:20, NIV)*
Life Principle	Simple trust requires only that the object of your trust be completely trustworthy. The LORD Jesus earned your trust on the cross where He died for your sins.
Life changes	_____ _____ _____ _____ _____ _____ _____ ⇨ ∞ 💭 📢 ⛪ ⊕ 🎯

June 15

God's Word	*The wise in heart are called discerning, and gracious words make a person persuasive.* *(Proverbs 16:21, NIV)*
Life Principle	If dogs could talk, would they compare your way of speaking to a golden retriever or a pit bull? Grace-filled speech will promote positive changes.
Life changes	_____ _____ _____ _____ _____ _____ _____ _____

June 16

God's Word	*A wise man's heart guides his mouth, and his lips promote instruction.* *(Proverbs 16:23, NIV)*
Life Principle	If unhelpful speech is normal for you, you cannot simply cover your mouth. You need a heart transplant. Change what is inside to get the right words outside.
Life changes	_____ _____ _____ _____ _____ _____ _____ _____

June 17

God's Word	*There is a way that seems right to a man, but in the end it leads to death.* *(Proverbs 16:25, NIV)*
Life Principle	*"Follow your heart,"* or *"Be the captain of your own ship"* – euphemisms for nothing less than pure selfishness. Jesus said, *"I am the Way"* and *"Follow Me!"*[a]
Life changes	_____ _____ _____ _____ _____ _____ _____ ⇨ ∞ 💭 📢 ⌂ ⊕ 🎯

[a] Ref. John 14:1; Matthew 4:19.

June 18

God's Word	*The laborer's appetite works for him; his hunger drives him on. (Proverbs 16:26, NIV)*
Life Principle	Ultimately you work to provide for the necessities of life. Take away this incentive and you can become lazy and demanding.
Life changes	_____ _____ _____ _____ _____ _____ _____ _____

June 19

God's Word	*A perverse man stirs up dissension, and a gossip separates close friends. (Proverbs 16:28, NIV)*
Life Principle	Your relationships are so important to God that those who cause strife and divisions are called "perverse."
Life changes	_____ _____ _____ _____ _____ _____ _____ _____ ⇨ ∞ 💭 📢 🔼 ⊕ 🎯

June 20

God's Word	*Gray hair is a crown of splendor; it is attained by a righteous life.* *(Proverbs 16:31, NIV)*
Life Principle	Consider a direct benefit of doing what is right in God's eyes: it keeps you from doing the dumb things that can cut short your years.
Life changes	_____ _____ _____ _____ _____ _____ _____ _____

June 21

God's Word	*Better a patient man than a warrior, a man who controls his temper than one who takes a city.* *(Proverbs 16:32, NIV)*
Life Principle	Anyone can lose control and blow up. Strength of body or strength of character – both take disciplined work. Will you commit to work on patience?
Life changes	_____ _____ _____ _____ _____ _____ _____ _____

June 22

God's Word	Better a dry crust with peace and quiet than a house full of feasting, with strife. (Proverbs 17:1, NIV)
Life Principle	Set your priority on building and maintaining good relationships with other people. You may not become rich but your life will be satisfying.
Life changes	_____ _____ _____ _____ _____ _____ _____ _____ ⇨ ∞ 💭 📢 ☝ ⊕ 🎯

June 23

God's Word	The crucible for silver and the furnace for gold, but the LORD tests the heart. (Proverbs 17:3, NIV)
Life Principle	God knows everything. So there is no point trying to hide something from Him. Be honest and let Him test your attitudes and actions.
Life changes	_____ _____ _____ _____ _____ _____ _____ _____ ⇨ ∞ 💭 ◁ ⛏ ⊕ 🎯

June 24

God's Word	*He who mocks the poor shows contempt for their Maker; whoever gloats over disaster will not go unpunished.* *(Proverbs 17:5, NIV)*
Life Principle	Does it really make sense to look down on people less fortunate than you? Think about it – no matter how much you have, someone else has more.
Life changes	_____ _____ _____ _____ _____ _____ _____

June 25

God's Word	*Children's children are a crown to the aged, and parents are the pride of their children. (Proverbs 17:6, NIV)*
Life Principle	Family values include: Grandparents valuing their grandchildren. Parents valuing their children. Children valuing their parents. Value your family!
Life changes	_____ _____ _____ _____ _____ _____ _____

June 26

God's Word	*He who covers over an offense promotes love, but whoever repeats the matter separates close friends. (Proverbs 17:9, NIV)*
Life Principle	Choose your battles wisely. Not every offense is worth calling out. And no personal offense is worth calling out to others. Keep it personal.
Life changes	_____ _____ _____ _____ _____ _____ _____

June 27

God's Word	*A rebuke impresses a man of discernment more than a hundred lashes a fool. (Proverbs 17:10, NIV)*
Life Principle	You can evaluate good character with ease: issue a fair rebuke and watch the reaction you get. By the way, how do you react to correction?
Life changes	_____ _____ _____ _____ _____ _____ _____ _____

June 28

God's Word	*If a man pays back evil for good, evil will never leave his house.* *(Proverbs 17:13, NIV)*
Life Principle	The Bible is clear: you will reap what you sow.[b] The reaping will come later and will be greater than what you sow. Be sure to sow good seed throughout life.
Life changes	_____ _____ _____ _____ _____ _____ _____

[b] Ref. Galatians 6:7.

June 29

God's Word	*Acquitting the guilty and condemning the innocent— the LORD detests them both. (Proverbs 17:15, NIV)*
Life Principle	God enacts justice. He has also instilled in each of us a longing for justice. Be honest and objective in rendering judgments about the actions of others.
Life changes	_____ _____ _____ _____ _____ _____ _____

June 30

God's Word	A friend loves at all times, and a brother is born for adversity. (Proverbs 17:17, NIV)
Life Principle	Some people are difficult to love. Some even refuse your love. Yet our calling is to love one another – no limit and no conditions.
Life changes	

July

The proverbs of Solomon
son of David, king of Israel: ... for
giving prudence to the simple ...
(Proverbs 1:1,4, NIV)

Symbol	Life Change
⇨	A command to follow
∞	A principle to use
💭	Thoughts to engage and attitudes to avoid
📢	What you say and how you say it
⚒	A good work to start
✦	A sin to confess and forsake
🎯	Thanksgiving for God's hand at work in your life

July 1

God's Word	*He who loves a quarrel loves sin; he who builds a high gate invites destruction. (Proverbs 17:19, NIV)*
Life Principle	Some people seem to enjoy fighting more than getting along. Such behavior hurts people and is rightly called sin. Are you inviting destruction through strife?
Life changes	_____ _____ _____ _____ _____ _____ _____

July 2

God's Word	*A cheerful heart is good medicine, but a crushed spirit dries up the bones. (Proverbs 17:22, NIV)*
Life Principle	A cheerful heart heals body and soul far better than a broken spirit. Find joy by focusing on the grace and strength the LORD gives and will not take away.
Life changes	_____ _____ _____ _____ _____ _____ _____

July 3

God's Word	*A wicked man accepts a bribe in secret to pervert the course of justice. (Proverbs 17:23, NIV)*
Life Principle	Any nation of laws can be subverted by those who use money to avoid judgment. Justice depends on people who ignore bribes in order to do what is right.
Life changes	_____ _____ _____ _____ _____ _____ _____ _____

July 4

God's Word	*A discerning man keeps wisdom in view, but a fool's eyes wander to the ends of the earth. (Proverbs 17:24, NIV)*
Life Principle	What is it that holds your interest these days? Are your eyes looking in the right places for the right things? So easy it is to wander from God's truth.
Life changes	_____ _____ _____ _____ _____ _____ _____ ⇨ ∞ 💭 📢 ☝ ⊕ 🎯

July 5

God's Word	*A man of knowledge uses words with restraint, and ... is even-tempered. Even a fool is thought wise if he keeps silent...* *(Proverbs 17:27-28, NIV)*
Life Principle	The next time someone does something that rips your heart out – remember to hold your tongue. Better to cool down and think straight before you act.
Life changes	_____ _____ _____ _____ _____ _____ _____

July 6

God's Word	*An unfriendly man pursues selfish ends; he defies all sound judgment.* *(Proverbs 18:1, NIV)*
Life Principle	In God's economy, thinking only of your self is not logical. Selfishness, in effect, breeds craziness.
Life changes	_____ _____ _____ _____ _____ _____ _____ _____

July 7

God's Word	*When wickedness comes, so does contempt, and with shame comes disgrace. (Proverbs 18:3, NIV)*
Life Principle	The world has deliberately removed shame from the public forum. People make *mistakes* or *life-choices* but nothing is considered shameful. Really?
Life changes	_____ _____ _____ _____ _____ _____ _____ _____

July 8

God's Word	It is not good to be partial to the wicked or to deprive the innocent of justice. (Proverbs 18:5, NIV)
Life Principle	Any group of people, to endure, must enact justice. This means standing up for the weak and standing up to the wicked.
Life changes	_____ _____ _____ _____ _____ _____ _____ _____ _____

July 9

God's Word	*The words of a gossip are like choice morsels; they go down to a man's inmost parts.* *(Proverbs 18:8, NIV)*
Life Principle	The latest news is often nothing more than gossip. Would you say it if the person involved was listening? If not, say it not.
Life changes	_____ _____ _____ _____ _____ _____ _____

July 10

God's Word	One who is slack in his work is brother to one who destroys. (Proverbs 18:9, NIV)
Life Principle	A lazy worker hurts more than just himself. Other workers have to fill the void and become discouraged. Soon the whole operation flounders.
Life changes	_____ _____ _____ _____ _____ _____ _____ _____

July 11

God's Word	*The wealth of the rich is their fortified city; they imagine it an unscalable wall.* *(Proverbs 18:11, NIV)*
Life Principle	As many winners of extremely large lotteries have demonstrated, there is no amount of money so large it cannot be lost. True security is in God alone.
Life changes	_____ _____ _____ _____ _____ _____ _____ _____ ⇨ ∞ 💭 📣 ☝ ⊕ 🎯

July 12

God's Word	Before his downfall a man's heart is proud, but humility comes before honor. (Proverbs 18:12, NIV)
Life Principle	Ironically, pride is the way down while humility is the way up. Puffing yourself up only brings you down in the end. Humble service will result in honor.
Life changes	_____ _____ _____ _____ _____ _____ _____ _____

July 13

God's Word	*He who answers before listening—that is his folly and his shame.* *(Proverbs 18:13, NIV)*
Life Principle	Do you tend to formulate your reply while the other person is still speaking? Focus on understanding well enough so you can summarize what was said.
Life changes	_____ _____ _____ _____ _____ _____ _____ _____

July 14

God's Word	*A gift opens the way for the giver and ushers him into the presence of the great. (Proverbs 18:16 , NIV)*
Life Principle	Similar to the effect of a bribe, your personal gifts/talents open doors for you. Work hard to improve in your area of giftedness. People will notice.
Life changes	_____ _____ _____ _____ _____ _____ _____ _____ ⇨ ∞ 💭 📣 ✋ ⊕ 🎯

July 15

God's Word	*The first to present his case seems right, till another comes forward and questions him.* *(Proverbs 18:17, NIV)*
Life Principle	Never rush to judgment. You really need to hear both sides of an issue to discern the truth.
Life changes	_____ _____ _____ _____ _____ _____ _____ _____

July 16

God's Word	*An offended brother is more unyielding than a fortified city, and disputes are like the barred gates of a citadel. (Proverbs 18:19, NIV)*
Life Principle	When someone holds something against you, they might as well be in a walled city. It is up to you to scale the wall. Name your offense and seek forgiveness.
Life changes	_____ _____ _____ _____ _____ _____ _____

July 17

God's Word	*The tongue has the power of life and death, and those who love it will eat its fruit. (Proverbs 18:21, NIV)*
Life Principle	Do you realize the power of words? You can use them to lift up and encourage others from the brink of death ... or your words can push them over the edge.
Life changes	_____ _____ _____ _____ _____ _____ _____ _____

July 18

God's Word	*He who finds a wife finds what is good and receives favor from the Lord. (Proverbs 18:22, NIV)*
Life Principle	Should you live together instead of getting married? Only if you want to miss a great blessing. God has established great value in the institution of marriage.
Life changes	_____ _____ _____ _____ _____ _____ _____ _____ ⇨ ∞ 💭 📣 ☝ ⊕ 🎯

July 19

God's Word	*A man of many companions may come to ruin, but there is a friend who sticks closer than a brother.* *(Proverbs 18;24, NIV)*
Life Principle	Do you have a good friend – a "no matter what happens" friend? Jesus said, "*And surely I am with you always, to the very end of the age*" *(Matthew 28:20, NIV).*
Life changes	_____ _____ _____ _____ _____ _____ _____ _____ ⇨ ∞ 💭 ◁ 🔥 ⊕ 🎯

July 20

God's Word	*Better a poor man whose walk is blameless than a fool whose lips are perverse. (Proverbs 19:1, NIV)*
Life Principle	Life can take everything away from you but your integrity. Cling to it – never give it away through careless words or deeds.
Life changes	_____ _____ _____ _____ _____ _____ _____ _____

July 21

God's Word	*A man's own folly ruins his life, yet his heart rages against the Lord. (Proverbs 19:3, NIV)*
Life Principle	Folly arises from your lack of forethought. Bad consequences arise from your foolish choices. Can you seriously blame God for the outcome?
Life changes	_____ _____ _____ _____ _____ _____ _____ _____

July 22

God's Word	*A false witness will not go unpunished, and he who pours out lies will not go free.* (Proverbs 19:5, NIV)
Life Principle	Lying to people is bad enough. Lying under oath in a court case should get you the penalty you were trying to inflict on the accused.
Life changes	_____ _____ _____ _____ _____ _____ _____ _____

July 23

God's Word	*...Everyone is the friend of a man who gives gifts. A poor man is shunned by all his relatives—how much more do his friends avoid him! (Proverbs 19:6-7, NIV)*
Life Principle	If you show preference to those with money and shun those less fortunate, have you not made money an idol?
Life changes	

July 24

God's Word	*A man's wisdom gives him patience; it is to his glory to overlook an offense. (Proverbs 19:11, NIV)*
Life Principle	If you want patience (*and you want it now*), start thinking. Wisdom gives you perspective to measure offenses in God's economy rather than your own.
Life changes	_____ _____ _____ _____ _____ _____ _____ _____

July 25

God's Word	*A foolish son is his father's ruin, and a quarrelsome wife is like a constant dripping. (Proverbs 19:13, NIV)*
Life Principle	It is well established that no one is perfect. That means that everyone, at some point, will let you down. Prepare yourself now to avoid devastation later.
Life changes	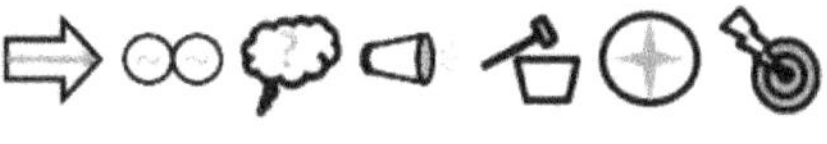

July 26

God's Word	*Laziness brings on deep sleep, and the shiftless man goes hungry.* *(Proverbs 19:15, NIV)*
Life Principle	Sleep is good when it is driven by a sense of purpose and a job well done.
Life changes	_____ _____ _____ _____ _____ _____ _____ _____ _____

July 27

God's Word	*He who is kind to the poor lends to the Lord, and he will reward him for what he has done. (Proverbs 19:17, NIV)*
Life Principle	When you love the LORD, you share His concern for the poor. Your gift to those less fortunate is really an investment that yields a return in God's kingdom.
Life changes	_____ _____ _____ _____ _____ _____ _____ _____

July 28

God's Word	*A hot-tempered man must pay the penalty; if you rescue him, you will have to do it again. (Proverbs 19:19, NIV)*
Life Principle	Anger leads to many miseries, even murder (Matthew 5:21-22). Angry people must suffer the consequences to avoid more serious problems later.
Life changes	_____ _____ _____ _____ _____ _____ _____

July 29

God's Word	*Many are the plans in a man's heart, but it is the Lord's purpose that prevails. (Proverbs 19:21, NIV)*
Life Principle	It is comforting to know that no matter how hard you plan and pray, God is always working for what He knows is best for you.
Life changes	_____ _____ _____ _____ _____ _____ _____ _____

July 30

God's Word	*The fear of the Lord leads to life: Then one rests content, untouched by trouble. (Proverbs 19:23, NIV)*
Life Principle	Your security rests in a good relationship with the LORD. Trouble will eventually come to you – but you will never face it alone.
Life changes	_____ _____ _____ _____ _____ _____ _____ _____

July 31

God's Word	*Flog a mocker, and the simple will learn prudence; rebuke a discerning man, and he will gain knowledge. (Proverbs 19:25, NIV)*
Life Principle	Correction is never easy but it has a positive effect in the end. The rebellious mocker is silenced. And a wise man gets wiser still.
Life changes	_____ _____ _____ _____ _____ _____ _____ _____

August

> The proverbs of Solomon
> son of David, king of Israel: ... for
> giving ... knowledge ... to the young.
> (Proverbs 1:1,4, NIV)

Symbol	Life Change
⇨	A command to follow
∞	A principle to use
(?)	Thoughts to engage and attitudes to avoid
📢	What you say and how you say it
⚒	A good work to start
✦	A sin to confess and forsake
🎯	Thanksgiving for God's hand at work in your life

August 1

God's Word	*Stop listening to instruction, my son and you will stray from the words of knowledge.* *(Proverbs 19:27, NIV)*
Life Principle	God is speaking to you even now – the Bible is His word written to you and for you. When you read the Bible, read it like a letter to you from your Father in Heaven.
Life changes	_____ _____ _____ _____ _____ _____ _____

August 2

God's Word	*A corrupt witness mocks at justice, and the mouth of the wicked gulps down evil. (Proverbs 19:28, NIV)*
Life Principle	Justice is based on a righteous standard. A witness who lies to cheat the system deprives everyone of justice. Justice demands truth.
Life changes	_____ _____ _____ _____ _____ _____ _____ _____

August 3

God's Word	*Wine is a mocker and beer a brawler; whoever is led astray by them is not wise. (Proverbs 20:1, NIV)*
Life Principle	Too much of anything is generally not wise. So it is with alcohol. It can easily take control of your life. Be smart and temperate.
Life changes	⇨ ∞ 💬 ◁ ⌂ ⊕ 🎯

August 4

God's Word	*It is to a man's honor to avoid strife, but every fool is quick to quarrel. (Proverbs 20:3, NIV)*
Life Principle	Just as a boxer parries many blows before he counter-punches, you must choose the right time to fight. Only fight the important battles.
Life changes	_____ _____ _____ _____ _____ _____ _____ _____ ⇨ ∞ 💭 📢 ⛏ ⊕ 🎯

August 5

God's Word	*A sluggard does not plow in season; so at harvest time he looks but finds nothing. (Proverbs 20:4, NIV)*
Life Principle	A farmer does not harvest the fruit of his labors – without the labor. It is time to stop dreaming and get to work.
Life changes	_____ _____ _____ _____ _____ _____ _____ _____ ⇨ ∞ 💭 📢 ⌂ ⊕ 🎯

August 6

God's Word	*Many a man claims to have unfailing love, but a faithful man who can find? (Proverbs 20:6, NIV)*
Life Principle	The world needs faithful people. Faithful people actually help others and bring hope to a cynical world. So be dependable to the people in your life.
Life changes	_____ _____ _____ _____ _____ _____ _____ _____ ⇨ ∞ 💭 📢 🔼 ⊕ 🎯

August 7

God's Word	*The righteous man leads a blameless life; blessed are his children after him. (Proverbs 20:7, NIV)*
Life Principle	Children watch and remember the things you do and say long after you have forgotten. Be the *example* that will bless them.
Life changes	_____ _____ _____ _____ _____ _____ _____ _____ ⇨ ∞ 💭 📢 🔼 ⊕ 🎯

August 8

God's Word	*Who can say, "I have kept my heart pure; I am clean and without sin"?* *(Proverbs 20:9, NIV)*
Life Principle	When someone accuses you, do you immediately proclaim your innocence? Or do you first take an honest look at your own actions and intent?
Life changes	_____ _____ _____ _____ _____ _____ _____ _____

August 9

God's Word	*Differing weights and differing measures—the Lord detests them both. (Proverbs 20:10, NIV)*
Life Principle	Your expectations of others should not be higher than the expectations you hold for yourself.
Life changes	_____ _____ _____ _____ _____ _____ _____

August 10

God's Word	*Even a child is known by his actions, by whether his conduct is pure and right. (Proverbs 20:11, NIV)*
Life Principle	Even the best of intentions are known only to you. The world judges your purity by what you say and do.
Life changes	_____ _____ _____ _____ _____ _____ _____ _____ ⇨ ∞ 🗨 📣 ⛄ ⊕ 🎯

August 11

God's Word	*Ears that hear and eyes that see—the Lord has made them both.* *(Proverbs 20:12, NIV)*
Life Principle	Since God gave you two ears and two eyes but only one mouth, how much time should you spend talking versus observing and listening?
Life changes	_____ _____ _____ _____ _____ _____ _____

August 12

God's Word	*Gold there is, and rubies in abundance, but lips that speak knowledge are a rare jewel. (Proverbs 20:15, NIV)*
Life Principle	There is a time to listen and a time to speak. Make sure your words count. Speak with honesty, compassion, and the wisdom of God.
Life changes	_____ _____ _____ _____ _____ _____ _____

August 13

God's Word	*Food gained by fraud tastes sweet to a man, but he ends up with a mouth full of gravel. (Proverbs 20:17, NIV)*
Life Principle	You may succeed in cheating others for a time. The reward may seem pleasant for a time. But the Spirit of God will never let you forget the one you hurt.
Life changes	_____ _____ _____ _____ _____ _____ _____ ⇨ ∞ 💭 📢 🔼 ⊕ 🎯

August 14

God's Word	*A gossip betrays a confidence; so avoid a man who talks too much. (Proverbs 20:19, NIV)*
Life Principle	A gossip is like wet sponge. No matter how closely you hold it, something is going to leak out. Far better to avoid talking to a gossip.
Life changes	_____ _____ _____ _____ _____ _____ _____ _____

August 15

God's Word	*An inheritance quickly gained at the beginning will not be blessed at the end. (Proverbs 20:21, NIV)*
Life Principle	Easy come, easy go. That is how it is with a windfall. If you do not have to work for it, you do not appreciate its value.
Life changes	_____ _____ _____ _____ _____ _____ _____ _____

August 16

God's Word	*Do not say, "I'll pay you back for this wrong!" Wait for the Lord, and he will deliver you. (Proverbs 20:22, NIV)*
Life Principle	The human desire for revenge is natural. And it is powerful. But the LORD is supernatural and all-powerful. Let Him judge and handle the situation.
Life changes	_____ _____ _____ _____ _____ _____ _____ _____

August 17

God's Word	*The Lord detests differing weights, and dishonest scales do not please him. (Proverbs 20:23, NIV)*
Life Principle	It is so easy to use a microscope to judge the actions and intent of others but be completely blind to your own faults. First, take a good look in the mirror.
Life changes	_____ _____ _____ _____ _____ _____ _____

August 18

God's Word	*It is a trap for a man to dedicate something rashly and only later to consider his vows. (Proverbs 20:25, NIV)*
Life Principle	The world needs promise-keepers not promise-makers.
Life changes	_____ _____ _____ _____ _____ _____ _____ _____ ⇨ ∞ 💭 📢 ☝ ⊕ 🎯

August 19

God's Word	A wise king winnows out the wicked; he drives the threshing wheel over them. (Proverbs 20:26, NIV)
Life Principle	In any company, church, or group, there will be some level of wickedness. It is sure to grow unless you take a stand against it.
Life changes	_____ _____ _____ _____ _____ _____ _____ _____

August 20

God's Word	Love and faithfulness keep a king safe; through love his throne is made secure. (Proverbs 20:28, NIV)
Life Principle	The greatest, most important command is to love God and love others (Mark 12:29-31). Faithfulness in this will give you both security and posterity.
Life changes	_____ _____ _____ _____ _____ _____ _____ _____

August 21

God's Word	*The glory of young men is their strength, gray hair the splendor of the old. (Proverbs 20:29, NIV)*
Life Principle	As a young person, you are strong and believe you will live forever. When you are old, you are wise and know better.
Life changes	_____ _____ _____ _____ _____ _____ _____

August 22

God's Word	*All a man's ways seem right to him, but the Lord weighs the heart. (Proverbs 21:2, NIV)*
Life Principle	If you have to rationalize your behavior to accept it, you have probably stepped over the line. God's righteous standard has no loopholes.
Life changes	_____ _____ _____ _____ _____ _____ _____ ⇨ ∞ 🗯 📢 ⛄ ⊕ 🎯

August 23

God's Word	*To do what is right and just is more acceptable to the Lord than sacrifice. (Proverbs 21:3, NIV)*
Life Principle	You can sacrifice much time and energy trying to make up for past indiscretions. Or you can accept God's forgiveness in Christ and simply follow Him.
Life changes	

August 24

God's Word	*The plans of the diligent lead to profit as surely as haste leads to poverty. (Proverbs 21:5, NIV)*
Life Principle	Whether it is finding a job or a mate or a rich spiritual life, anything worthwhile takes a good plan to succeed.
Life changes	_____ _____ _____ _____ _____ _____ _____ _____

August 25

God's Word	*The way of the guilty is devious, but the conduct of the innocent is upright. (Proverbs 21:8, NIV)*
Life Principle	You have to walk a continuously crooked path to avoid getting caught. Better to walk in righteousness where the path is straight and true.
Life changes	_____ _____ _____ _____ _____ _____ _____ _____

August 26

God's Word	*Better to live on a corner of the roof than share a house with a quarrelsome wife. (Proverbs 21:9, NIV)*
Life Principle	Marriage is a love relationship between three people – you, your spouse, and the LORD. Are you missing someone in your marriage?
Life changes	_____ _____ _____ _____ _____ _____ _____ _____ ⇨ ∞ 💭 📢 🛐 ⊕ 🎯

August 27

God's Word	*The Righteous One takes note of the house of the wicked and brings the wicked to ruin. (Proverbs 21:12, NIV)*
Life Principle	You cannot escape God's judgment. It may be delayed for a time. But judgment day is coming. Stop running and find God's grace while there is time.
Life changes	_____ _____ _____ _____ _____ _____ _____

August 28

God's Word	If a man shuts his ears to the cry of the poor, he too will cry out and not be answered. (Proverbs 21:13, NIV)
Life Principle	God's concern for the poor runs throughout the Bible. There will always be some who are poor (Matthew 26:11). Will you help to wipe their tears?
Life changes	_____ _____ _____ _____ _____ _____ _____

August 29

God's Word	*When justice is done, it brings joy to the righteous but terror to evildoers. (Proverbs 21:15, NIV)*
Life Principle	Justice is getting what you deserve. Mercy is not getting what you deserve. Which will serve to deter future evil?
Life changes	_____ _____ _____ _____ _____ _____ _____ _____

August 30

God's Word	He who loves pleasure `will become poor; whoever loves wine and oil will never be rich. (Proverbs 21:17, NIV)
Life Principle	To achieve your heart's desire requires hard work and persistence. There is no free lunch, no easy path, and no shortcut.
Life changes	_____ _____ _____ _____ _____ _____ _____ ⇨ ∞ 💭 ◁ 📤 ⊕ 🎯

August 31

God's Word	*In the house of the wise are stores of choice food and oil, but a foolish man devours all he has. (Proverbs 21:20, NIV)*
Life Principle	It seems obvious that consuming all you have will leave you with nothing. Why, then, do so many consume more than they have?
Life changes	

September

The proverbs of Solomon
son of David, king of Israel: ... for
giving ... discretion to the young.
(Proverbs 1:1,4, NIV)

Symbol	Life Change
	A command to follow
	A principle to use
	Thoughts to engage and attitudes to avoid
	What you say and how you say it
	A good work to start
	A sin to confess and forsake
	Thanksgiving for God's hand at work in your life

September 1

God's Word	*He who guards his mouth and his tongue keeps himself from calamity.* *(Proverbs 21:23, NIV)*
Life Principle	Practice engaging your mind before mouth. If what you are about to say is truthful, compassionate, and wise, then say it.
Life changes	_____ _____ _____ _____ _____ _____ _____ _____

September 2

God's Word	*The sluggard's craving will be the death of him …. All day long he craves for more, but the righteous give without sparing. (Proverbs 21:25-26, NIV)*
Life Principle	The sluggard wants and the righteous give - but not necessarily to the sluggard. Remember: "If a man will not work, he shall not eat" (2 Thess. 3:10, NIV).
Life changes	_____ _____ _____ _____ _____ _____ _____ _____ ⇨ ∞ 💭 📢 ☝ ⊕ 🎯

September 3

God's Word	*There is no wisdom, no insight, no plan that can succeed against the Lord. (Proverbs 21:30, NIV)*
Life Principle	Since God is God, you cannot outthink Him, outsmart Him, or outmaneuver Him. Your best plan is to humbly follow Him.
Life changes	_____ _____ _____ _____ _____ _____ _____ _____

September 4

God's Word	A good name is more desirable than great riches; to be esteemed is better than silver or gold. (Proverbs 22:1, NIV)
Life Principle	A great name reflects fame – one known among people. A good name reflects righteousness – one known by God. Seek first His kingdom!
Life changes	_____ _____ _____ _____ _____ _____ _____ _____

September 5

God's Word	*Rich and poor have this in common: The Lord is the Maker of them all. (Proverbs 22:2, NIV)*
Life Principle	No one is more important than the next. Each person is special - uniquely made by God. No two people are alike. But the same God is LORD over all.
Life changes	_____ _____ _____ _____ _____ _____ _____ _____

September 6

God's Word	*In the paths of the wicked lie thorns and snares, but he who guards his soul stays far from them. (Proverbs 22:5, NIV)*
Life Principle	Walk alone and stumble. Walk with God and have a strong friend to lead you away from danger and catch you if you fall.
Life changes	_____ _____ _____ _____ _____ _____ _____ _____

September 7

God's Word	*Train a child in the way he should go, and when he is old he will not turn from it. (Proverbs 22:6, NIV)*
Life Principle	Teach your child to love God and love people. This gives your child the best possible start. But remember this is a principle - not a guarantee of good choices as an adult.
Life changes	_____ _____ _____ _____ _____ _____ _____ _____

September 8

God's Word	A generous man will himself be blessed, for he shares his food with the poor. (Proverbs 22:9, NIV)
Life Principle	Jesus said that every generation will have poor people (Mark 14:7). Therefore, there are always opportunities for you to be generous.
Life changes	_____ _____ _____ _____ _____ _____ _____ _____

September 9

God's Word	*He who loves a pure heart and whose speech is gracious will have the king for his friend.* *(Proverbs 22:11, NIV)*
Life Principle	Purity means something is the same inside and out. One who is pure of heart is obvious to everyone – speech and deeds that reflect the goodness of God.
Life changes	_____ _____ _____ _____ _____ _____ _____ _____

September 10

God's Word	The sluggard says, "There is a lion outside!" or, "I will be murdered in the streets!" (Proverbs 22:13, NIV)
Life Principle	What excuse keeps you pursuing God's will? Does fear keep you from making a difference in the lives of people?
Life changes	_____ _____ _____ _____ _____ _____ _____

September 11

God's Word	*Folly is bound up in the heart of a child, but the rod of discipline will drive it far from him. (Proverbs 22:15, NIV)*
Life Principle	No parent has to teach a child to say with defiance, "NO!" It is built-in to our nature. Correction and training in righteousness are essential.
Life changes	_____ _____ _____ _____ _____ _____ _____ _____

September 12

God's Word	Do not exploit the poor ... and do not crush the needy in court, for the Lord will take up their case ... (Proverbs 22:22-23, NIV)
Life Principle	An earthly judge can be corrupted by people with wealth. Be fair in your dealings with people or you will have no defense in God's courtroom.
Life changes	_____ _____ _____ _____ _____ _____ _____ _____ _____

September 13

God's Word	*Do not associate with one easily angered or you may learn his ways and get yourself ensnared.* *(Proverbs 22:24-25, NIV)*
Life Principle	Angry people cause division and hurt to those around them. Why hang out with someone like that?
Life changes	

September 14

God's Word	*Do not move an ancient boundary stone set up by your forefathers.* *(Proverbs 22:28, NI V)*
Life Principle	Show respect for your neighbors and their possessions. Respect breeds trust. Living in close proximity with anyone requires much trust.
Life changes	

September 15

God's Word	*When you sit to dine with a ruler, note well what is before you, and put a knife to your throat if you are given to gluttony. (Proverbs 23:1-2, NIV)*
Life Principle	In God's economy, eating too much is just as bad as drinking too much.
Life changes	_____ _____ _____ _____ _____ _____ _____

September 16

God's Word	*When you sit to dine with a ruler ... Do not crave his delicacies, for that food is deceptive.* *(Proverbs 23:1,3, NIV)*
Life Principle	A desire to get rich and enjoy luxury without working is common though harmful. It is not possible to put God and money first.
Life changes	_____ _____ _____ _____ _____ _____ _____ ⇨ ∞ 💭 📢 ⛊ ⊕ 🎯

September 17

God's Word	*Cast but a glance at riches, and they are gone, for they will surely sprout wings and fly off to the sky like an eagle. (Proverbs 23:5, NIV)*
Life Principle	All the money in the world will not make you secure. God is our Rock in whom we can always rely.
Life changes	⇨ ∞ 💭 ◁ 🖐 ⊕ 🎯

September 18

God's Word	*Do not eat the food of a stingy man, do not crave his delicacies; for he is the kind of man who is always thinking about the cost. (Proverbs 23:6-7, NIV)*
Life Principle	No one can enjoy what a stingy person has to offer. It always comes with strings attached.
Life changes	_____ _____ _____ _____ _____ _____ _____ ⇨ ∞ 💭 📢 ⛶ ⊕ 🎯

September 19

God's Word	*Do not speak to a fool, for he will scorn the wisdom of your words.* *(Proverbs 23:9, NIV)*
Life Principle	A fool is one who rejects the reality of our Creator God (Psalm 14:1). You will know a fool when he rejects your words and attacks your character for no reason.
Life changes	_____ _____ _____ _____ _____ _____ _____

September 20

God's Word	*Apply your heart to instruction and your ears to words of knowledge. (Proverbs 23:12, NIV)*
Life Principle	Both a sponge and a fountain take in water. But only one puts that water to good use. Seek to learn but also put what you know into practice.
Life changes	_____ _____ _____ _____ _____ _____ _____ _____ ⇨ ∞ 💭 ◁ 👆 ⊕ 🎯

September 21

God's Word	*Do not withhold discipline from a child; if you punish him with the rod, he will not die.* *(Proverbs 23:13, NIV)*
Life Principle	Never be afraid to correct a child who strays from the right path. Appropriate punishment helps the child see the boundaries around good behavior.
Life changes	_____ _____ _____ _____ _____ _____ _____ ⇨ ∞ 💭 📢 ⬆ ⊕ 🎯

September 22

God's Word	My son, if your heart is wise, then my heart will be glad; my inmost being will rejoice when your lips speak what is right. (Proverbs 23:15-16, NIV)
Life Principle	Think the right thoughts and do the right things. Maybe it seems old-fashioned. But it brings pleasure to the One who created you.
Life changes	_____ _____ _____ _____ _____ _____ _____ _____

September 23

God's Word	*Do not let your heart envy sinners, but always be zealous for the fear of the LORD. There is surely a future hope for you...* *(Proverbs 23:17-18, NIV)*
Life Principle	Hope is the fuel that propels you forward in life. Keep your eyes on the LORD and remember His promises. The wealth of those who despise Him does not last.
Life changes	_____ _____ _____ _____ _____ _____ _____ _____

September 24

God's Word	*Do not join those who drink too much wine or gorge themselves on meat, for drunkards and gluttons become poor ...* *(Proverbs 23:20-21, NIV)*
Life Principle	Life is expensive enough without the bill for a drunken feast. It costs you more than money: pain, bad decisions, embarrassment, and broken relationships.
Life changes	_____ _____ _____ _____ _____ _____ _____ _____

September 25

God's Word	*The father of a righteous man has great joy; he who has a wise son delights in him. May your father and mother be glad ... (Proverbs 23:24-25, NIV)*
Life Principle	Moms and dads should be the most special people in your life, people that you want to be proud of you. Make them glad by loving God and loving people.
Life changes	_____ _____ _____ _____ _____ _____ _____ _____

September 26

God's Word	*My son, give me your heart and let your eyes keep to my ways, for a prostitute is a deep pit and a wayward wife is a narrow well. (Proverbs 23:26-27, NIV)*
Life Principle	Sexual temptation can change a person's theology more profoundly than a thousand of the best sermons ever preached. But illicit sex is a trap.
Life changes	_____ _____ _____ _____ _____ _____ _____ _____

September 27

God's Word	*Who has woe? Who has sorrow? ... Who has needless bruises? Who has bloodshot eyes? Those who linger over wine. (Proverbs 23:29-30, NIV)*
Life Principle	Woes and sorrows come to those who cede control to intoxicating drinks. Alcohol can be a ruthless master of your life. The fruit of the Holy Spirit is self-control.
Life changes	_____ _____ _____ _____ _____ _____ _____ _____ ⇨ ∞ 💭 📢 ⛊ ⊕ 🎯

September 28

God's Word	*Do not gaze at wine when it is red, when it sparkles in the cup, when it goes down smoothly! In the end it bites like a snake ...* *(Proverbs 23:31-32, NIV)*
Life Principle	Looking for answers to life's problems in a strong drink? Look again to a far better source. Jesus said, *"I am the Way and the Truth and the Life"* (John 14:1, NIV).
Life changes	_____ _____ _____ _____ _____ _____ _____ _____

September 29

God's Word	*Do not envy wicked men ... for their hearts plot violence, and their lips talk about making trouble.* *(Proverbs 24:1-2, NIV)*
Life Principle	Never give the ideas of troublemakers any consideration. They may get the outcome you want but not in the way that pleases God.
Life changes	_____ _____ _____ _____ _____ _____ _____ _____ ⇨ ∞ 🗩 ◁ ⌂ ⊕ 🎯

September 30

God's Word	*By wisdom a house is built, and through understanding it is established.* *(Proverbs 24:3, NIV)*
Life Principle	God provides the solid foundation for building and securing a life that matters. His wisdom is found in His word, the Bible.
Life changes	_____ _____ _____ _____ _____ _____ _____

October

The proverbs of Solomon son of David, king of Israel: ... let the wise listen and add to their learning ... (Proverbs 1:1,5, NIV)

Symbol	Life Change
⇨	A command to follow
∞	A principle to use
💭?	Thoughts to engage and attitudes to avoid
📢	What you say and how you say it
⚒	A good work to start
✦	A sin to confess and forsake
🎯	Thanksgiving for God's hand at work in your life

October 1

God's Word	*For waging war you need guidance, and for victory many advisers. (Proverbs 24:6, NIV)*
Life Principle	Big decisions should not be made alone - seek the advice of wise and trusted friends. Then take the issue to the LORD in prayer. He is your best Advisor.
Life changes	_____ _____ _____ _____ _____ _____ _____

October 2

God's Word	*The schemes of folly are sin, and men detest a mocker. (Proverbs 24:9, NIV)*
Life Principle	It is always good to plan before you act – unless you are planning ungodly acts. If you ponder evil, you will eventually act on it.
Life changes	_____ _____ _____ _____ _____ _____ _____ _____ ⇨ ∞ 💭 📢 🔼 ⊕ 🎯

October 3

God's Word	*If you falter in times of trouble, how small is your strength! (Proverbs 24:10, NIV)*
Life Principle	God is our refuge and strength (Psalm 46:1). If you rely on Him, no matter how small your faith may seem, your strength is great.
Life changes	_____ _____ _____ _____ _____ _____ _____

October 4

God's Word	Does not he who guards your life know it? Will he not repay each person according to what he has done? (Proverbs 24:12b, NIV)
Life Principle	Any parent fights the hardest when their child is threatened. How much harder do you think God will fight for you, the one to whom He gave life?
Life changes	_____ _____ _____ _____ _____ _____ _____ _____

October 5

God's Word	*Though a righteous man falls seven times, he rises again, but the wicked are brought down by calamity. (Proverbs 24:16, NIV)*
Life Principle	Nothing can happen to a child of God that does not first pass through the filter of His love for you and His knowledge of everything.
Life changes	

October 6

God's Word	*Do not gloat when your enemy falls; ... or the LORD will see and disapprove and turn his wrath away from him.* *(Proverbs 24:17-18, NIV)*
Life Principle	God loves each one of us because He is our Creator. Remember, in this world we are not really fighting against people but fighting for God's truth.
Life changes	_____ _____ _____ _____ _____ _____ _____ _____

October 7

God's Word	*Fear the LORD and the king, my son, and do not join with the rebellious, for those two will send sudden destruction upon them...* *(Proverbs 24:21-22, NIV)*
Life Principle	To fear (*revere, obey*) the LORD should be obvious. Since God ordains human government, show respect for leadership and obey the laws of the land.
Life changes	_____ _____ _____ _____ _____ _____ _____ _____

October 8

God's Word	Whoever says to the guilty, "You are innocent" peoples will curse him ... But it will go well with those who convict the guilty... (Proverbs 24:24-25, NIV)
Life Principle	Righteousness demands that justice prevail. Justice requires fair, impartial, and even-handed treatment of all people.
Life changes	_____ _____ _____ _____ _____ _____ _____ _____ _____

October 9

God's Word	*An honest answer is like a kiss on the lips.* *(Proverbs 24:26, NIV)*
Life Principle	A kiss on the lips is an intimate moment of contact between two people that liberates the relationship. Sharing the truth is equally intimate and liberating.
Life changes	_____ _____ _____ _____ _____ _____ _____ _____

October 10

God's Word	Do not testify against your neighbor without cause, or use your lips to deceive. (Proverbs 24:28, NIV)
Life Principle	A community depends on people generally getting along and working things out peaceably when there is conflict. Lies and deceit will ruin any community.
Life changes	

October 11

God's Word	*A little sleep, a little slumber … and poverty will come on you like a bandit and scarcity like an armed man. (Proverbs 24:33-34, NIV)*
Life Principle	Being unproductive is unprofitable. And laziness is a learned behavior. So take time off from time to time to recharge – but be careful not to learn laziness.
Life changes	_____ _____ _____ _____ _____ _____ _____ _____

October 12

God's Word	*Remove the dross from the silver, and out comes material for the silversmith ... (Proverbs 25:4, NIV)*
Life Principle	Remove the impurities and what remains is pure – the same inside and out. This can apply to your personal attitudes, a work group, and even a church.
Life changes	_____ _____ _____ _____ _____ _____ _____

October 13

God's Word	*Do not exalt yourself in the king's presence ... it is better for him to say to you, "Come up here," than ... to humiliate you before a nobleman. (Proverbs 25:6-7, NIV)*
Life Principle	Honor granted beats honor demanded any day of the week.
Life changes	_____ _____ _____ _____ _____ _____ _____ _____ ⇨ ∞ 💭 📢 ⛏ ⊕ 🎯

October 14

God's Word	*Do not betray another man's confidence, or he who hears it may shame you and you will never lose your bad reputation.* *(Proverbs 25:9-10, NIV)*
Life Principle	Once an idle word gets out, you cannot get it back. Relationships require trust. If you are told something in confidence, keep it to yourself.
Life changes	_____ _____ _____ _____ _____ _____ _____ _____

October 15

God's Word	*A word aptly spoken is like apples of gold in settings of silver.* *(Proverbs 25:11, NIV)*
Life Principle	The right word spoken the right way at the right time to the right person can right wrongs, win hearts, and move mountains.
Life changes	_____ _____ _____ _____ _____ _____ _____

October 16

God's Word	*Like clouds and wind without rain is a man who boasts of gifts he does not give.* *(Proverbs 25:14, NIV)*
Life Principle	A blustery boast is nothing but stale air. People remember what you do for them, not what you say you will do for them.
Life changes	_____ _____ _____ _____ _____ _____ _____ ⇨ ∞ 💭 📣 👍 ⊕ 🎯

October 17

God's Word	*Through patience a ruler can be persuaded, and a gentle tongue can break a bone.* *(Proverbs 25:15 , NIV)*
Life Principle	When you nag someone you usually get nowhere. But godly wisdom delivered with gentleness and respect can break through the walls that people erect.
Life changes	_____ _____ _____ _____ _____ _____ _____ _____

October 18

God's Word	*Like a bad tooth or a lame foot is reliance on the unfaithful in times of trouble. (Proverbs 25:19, NIV)*
Life Principle	Your feet take you 80,000 miles in your lifetime. Imagine the journey if even one foot is injured. This is how God feels when you break your promise to Him.
Life changes	_____ _____ _____ _____ _____ _____ _____ _____

October 19

God's Word	*If your enemy is hungry, give him food to eat; if ... thirsty, give him water to drink. In doing this, you will heap burning coals on his head... (Proverbs 25:21-22, NIV)*
Life Principle	Back then, fire was shared by carrying coals in a bowl on their head. It was an important need. Try blessing your enemies with more than they deserve.
Life changes	_____ _____ _____ _____ _____ _____ _____ ⇨ ∞ 💭 ◁ ⌂ ⊕ 🎯

October 20

God's Word	*Better to live on a corner of the roof than share a house with a quarrelsome wife. (Proverbs 25:24, NIV)*
Life Principle	A home can be ruined by conflict. Do not push the people you love out of the house. Temper your anger with patience and understanding.
Life changes	_____ _____ _____ _____ _____ _____ _____ _____ ⇨ ∞ 💭 📢 ⛊ ⊕ 🎯

October 21

God's Word	*Like a muddied spring or a polluted well is a righteous man who gives way to the wicked.* *(Proverbs 25:26, NIV)*
Life Principle	A righteous person who will compromise the truth of God's word is useless.
Life changes	_____ _____ _____ _____ _____ _____ _____

October 22

God's Word	*It is not good to eat too much honey, nor is it honorable to seek one's own honor.* *(Proverbs 25:27, NIV)*
Life Principle	Too much honey will make you sick. Expecting others to honor you is a sick attitude. The LORD Jesus put others first and so should you.
Life changes	_____ _____ _____ _____ _____ _____ _____

October 23

God's Word	*Like a city whose walls are broken down is a man who lacks self-control.* *(Proverbs 25:28, NIV)*
Life Principle	A city with no walls is open to threats of all kinds. So is anyone who will not exercise self-control. You are a danger to yourself and everyone else.
Life changes	_____ _____ _____ _____ _____ _____ _____ ⇨ ∞ 💭 ◁ ☁ ⊕ 🎯

October 24

God's Word	Like a fluttering sparrow or a darting swallow, an undeserved curse does not come to rest. (Proverbs 26:2, NIV)
Life Principle	Cursing a good person is like throwing a boomerang. While you are watching to see if it hits the target, it returns and hits you from behind.
Life changes	_____ _____ _____ _____ _____ _____ _____

October 25

God's Word	*Do not answer a fool according to his folly, or you will be like him yourself. (Proverbs 26:4, NIV)*
Life Principle	Trying to unravel the facts of a fool's argument is like trying to untie the legendary Gordian's knot. Like the fool, you will only waste your time.
Life changes	_____ _____ _____ _____ _____ _____ _____ _____

October 26

God's Word	*Answer a fool according to his folly, or he will be wise in his own eyes.* *(Proverbs 26:5, NIV)*
Life Principle	There are times that the lies of a fool must be corrected to avoid leading more people astray. You can count on God's truth to shed light on any issue.
Life changes	_____ _____ _____ _____ _____ _____ _____

October 27

God's Word	*Like tying a stone in a sling is the giving of honor to a fool.* *(Proverbs 26:8, NIV)*
Life Principle	Many nations have discovered the burden of selecting a fool to lead. Leaders need wisdom and righteousness to govern effectively.
Life changes	_____ _____ _____ _____ _____ _____ _____ ⇨ ∞ 💭 📣 🔼 ⊕ 🎯

October 28

God's Word	*Like an archer who wounds at random is he who hires a fool or any passer-by. (Proverbs 26:10, NIV)*
Life Principle	Whether it is a paid position or a volunteer, do not try to fit a square peg in a round hole. A person is right for a position based on skills, experience, and disposition.
Life changes	

October 29

God's Word	*Do you see a man wise in his own eyes? There is more hope for a fool than for him. (Proverbs 26:12, NIV)*
Life Principle	One who is educated may think he knows everything. But truly wise people think they know nothing. Use what you know wisely – for the benefit of others.
Life changes	_____ _____ _____ _____ _____ _____ _____

October 30

God's Word	*The sluggard buries his hand in the dish; he is too lazy to bring it back to his mouth. (Proverbs 26:15, NIV)*
Life Principle	Never expect others to do for you what you can do for yourself. God has given you skills, experience, and opportunity so you can put them to good use.
Life changes	_____ _____ _____ _____ _____ _____ _____ _____

October 31

God's Word	*Like one who seizes a dog by the ears is a passer-by who meddles in a quarrel not his own.* *(Proverbs 26:17, NIV)*
Life Principle	It is a one thing to try and help resolve a conflict. That is good. But it is quite another to take sides or try to sway the outcome.
Life changes	_____ _____ _____ _____ _____ _____ _____ _____ ⇨ ∞ 💭 📣 🏺 ⊕ 🎯

November

> *The proverbs of Solomon son of David, king of Israel: ... let the discerning get guidance.*
> *(Proverbs 1:1,5, NIV)*

Symbol	Life Change
⇨	A command to follow
∞	A principle to use
🧠❓	Thoughts to engage and attitudes to avoid
📣	What you say and how you say it
🔨	A good work to start
✦	A sin to confess and forsake
🎯	Thanksgiving for God's hand at work in your life

November 1

God's Word	*Without wood a fire goes out; without gossip a quarrel dies down.* *(Proverbs 26:20, NIV)*
Life Principle	Gossip fuels a conflict just like dry wood fuels a fire. Ask yourself – would you spread the gossip if the person was present? If not, then be quiet.
Life changes	_____ _____ _____ _____ _____ _____ _____ _____

November 2

God's Word	*The words of a gossip are like choice morsels; they go down to a man's inmost parts.* *(Proverbs 26:22, NIV)*
Life Principle	Gossip spreads quickly because deep down we each want to know the secrets (and lies) about others. The next time gossip starts, put a stop to it.
Life changes	_____ _____ _____ _____ _____ _____ _____ ⇨ ∞ 🗨 📢 ☝ ⊕ ◎

November 3

God's Word	*A lying tongue hates those it hurts, and a flattering mouth works ruin.* *(Proverbs 26:28, NIV)*
Life Principle	It is just a "little white lie" you say. Lies divide us. When you deceive others, you prove that you hate them. You must speak the truth in love to love others.
Life changes	_____ _____ _____ _____ _____ _____ _____ ⇨ ∞ 🗩 ◁ 🕭 ⊕ ◎

November 4

God's Word	*Do not boast about tomorrow, for you do not know what a day may bring forth.* *(Proverbs 27:1, NIV)*
Life Principle	You depend on the grace of God for your next breath. So how can you presume to make any plans on your own? Make sure your plans are in line with God's will.
Life changes	_____ _____ _____ _____ _____ _____ _____ ⇨ ∞ 💭 📢 ⚱ ⊕ 🎯

November 5

God's Word	*Let another praise you, and not your own mouth; someone else, and not your own lips.* *(Proverbs 27:2, NIV)*
Life Principle	Praise from Heaven is far superior to praise from people. Just use your God-given abilities the best you can. God will always remember.
Life changes	_____ _____ _____ _____ _____ _____ _____ _____ ⇨ ∞ 💬 📢 🔥 ⊕ 🎯

November 6

God's Word	*Better is open rebuke than hidden love.* *(Proverbs 27:5, NIV)*
Life Principle	Though an open rebuke may embarrass, there may be some truth to what is said. But hidden love does absolutely nothing. Let your love be transparent.
Life changes	_____ _____ _____ _____ _____ _____ _____ _____

November 7

God's Word	*Wounds from a friend can be trusted, but an enemy multiplies kisses. (Proverbs 27:6, NIV)*
Life Principle	Beware the person who flatters you freely. The platitudes will ultimately come with a price.
Life changes	_____ _____ _____ _____ _____ _____ _____ _____

November 8

God's Word	Perfume and incense bring joy to the heart, and the pleasantness of one's friend springs from his earnest counsel. (Proverbs 27:9, NIV)
Life Principle	Everyone needs someone trustworthy to be their truth-teller. A word of wisdom delivered with compassion is sweet indeed!
Life changes	_____ _____ _____ _____ _____ _____ _____

November 9

God's Word	*The prudent see danger and take refuge, but the simple keep going and suffer for it. (Proverbs 27:12, NIV)*
Life Principle	As you walk through life, stay on the clear path. If you walk along the rocky edges, you will stumble and probably fall.
Life changes	_____ _____ _____ _____ _____ _____ _____ _____

November 10

God's Word	*A quarrelsome wife is like a constant dripping on a rainy day ...* *(Proverbs 27:15, NIV)*
Life Principle	When two people live together as husband and wife, some conflict is inevitable. There is no need to start your own.
Life changes	_____ _____ _____ _____ _____ _____ _____

November 11

God's Word	*As iron sharpens iron, so one man sharpens another. (Proverbs 27:17, NIV)*
Life Principle	Iron is a hard, dense metal that requires something equally hard to sharpen it. Men have a tough side as well and need other men to help them grow in faith.
Life changes	_____ _____ _____ _____ _____ _____ _____

November 12

God's Word	*As water reflects a face, so a man's heart reflects the man. (Proverbs 27:19, NIV)*
Life Principle	Is the heart that God sees in you the same one that your friends and family see? What is on the inside should reflect clearly on the outside.
Life changes	_____ _____ _____ _____ _____ _____ _____

November 13

God's Word	*The crucible for silver and the furnace for gold, but man is tested by the praise he receives.* *(Proverbs 27:21, NIV)*
Life Principle	It is nice to get a pat on the back for a job well done. Be careful not to let it go to your head. Pride is at the top of the seven deadly sins (Proverbs 6:16-19).
Life changes	_____ _____ _____ _____ _____ _____ _____

November 14

God's Word	*Be sure you know the condition of your flocks, give careful attention to your herds.* *(Proverbs 27:23, NIV)*
Life Principle	In your marriage, family, workplace, or church, pay close attention to relationships. Are they authentic? Are they loving? Are they truthful? Are they growing?
Life changes	_____ _____ _____ _____ _____ _____ _____ _____ ⇨ ∞ 💭 📣 👆 ⊕ 🎯

November 15

God's Word	*The wicked man flees though no one pursues, but the righteous are as bold as a lion.* *(Proverbs 28:1, NIV)*
Life Principle	Lions are so bold they sleep during the day and hunt during the night. Are you bold when your faith is challenged or do you run for no reason?
Life changes	_____ _____ _____ _____ _____ _____ _____ _____

November 16

God's Word	A ruler who oppresses the poor is like a driving rain that leaves no crops. (Proverbs 28:3, NIV)
Life Principle	One in charge of many has great privilege but also great responsibility. You cannot take from the poor without leaving them nothing.
Life changes	_____ _____ _____ _____ _____ _____ _____ _____

November 17

God's Word	*Evil men do not understand justice, but those who seek the LORD understand it fully. (Proverbs 28:5, NIV)*
Life Principle	What irony! Those who do not fear the LORD fear justice. Yet the righteous see the urgent need for God's perfect justice.
Life changes	_____ _____ _____ _____ _____ _____ _____

November 18

God's Word	*He who increases his wealth by exorbitant interest amasses it for another, who will be kind to the poor. (Proverbs 28:8, NIV)*
Life Principle	How can you enjoy wealth obtained by evil means? Know this - if you enrich yourself unjustly, God will deal with you justly.
Life changes	_____ _____ _____ _____ _____ _____ _____

November 19

God's Word	*A rich man may be wise in his own eyes, but a poor man who has discernment sees through him.* *(Proverbs 28:11, NIV)*
Life Principle	One who is rich usually has a much higher opinion of himself than those who know him well. But money can create an obstacle to honesty from your friends.
Life changes	_____ _____ _____ _____ _____ _____ _____ _____

November 20

God's Word	*He who conceals his sins does not prosper, but whoever confesses and renounces them finds mercy. (Proverbs 28:13, NIV)*
Life Principle	You can hide your sin from many people but never from God. The good news is that if you agree with God that it is wrong and renounce it, you will find a merciful God.
Life changes	_____ _____ _____ _____ _____ _____ _____

November 21

God's Word	*Blessed is the man who always fears the LORD, but he who hardens his heart falls into trouble.* *(Proverbs 28:14, NIV)*
Life Principle	*Is my way better than God's way?* The moment that you think your way is better, your hard heart stops listening to God.
Life changes	_____ _____ _____ _____ _____ _____ _____ _____

November 22

God's Word	*He who hates ill-gotten gain will enjoy a long life. (Proverbs 28;16, NIV)*
Life Principle	When you seek what is not right for you to have, you jeopardize your remaining years. Pursuing godly goals allows you to enjoy a long, productive life.
Life changes	_____ _____ _____ _____ _____ _____ _____ _____

November 23

God's Word	*He whose walk is blameless is kept safe but he whose ways are perverse will suddenly fall.* *(Proverbs 28:18, NIV)*
Life Principle	A ship will leave behind a wake that other boats will encounter – either calm or turbulent. What kind of wake will your life leave for others?
Life changes	

November 24

God's Word	*He who works his land will have abundant food, but the one who chases fantasies will have his fill of poverty. (Proverbs 28:19, NIV)*
Life Principle	Dreams can inspire and motivate. But dreams will never be realized without hard work.
Life changes	_____ _____ _____ _____ _____ _____ _____

November 25

God's Word	*To show partiality is not good — yet a man will do wrong for a piece of bread. (Proverbs 28:21, NIV)*
Life Principle	God sends sunshine and rain to the righteous and the unrighteous. Since God shows love to every person, is it right for you to show partiality to anyone?
Life changes	_____ _____ _____ _____ _____ _____ _____

November 26

God's Word	*He who robs his father or mother and says, "It's not wrong" — he is partner to him who destroys. (Proverbs 28:24, NIV)*
Life Principle	The family unit is the key to a stable society. When you fail to honor your parents, you rob them of their God-given dignity and initiate a destructive cycle for all.
Life changes	_____ _____ _____ _____ _____ _____ _____

November 27

God's Word	*He who trusts in himself is a fool, but he who walks in wisdom is kept safe. (Proverbs 28:26, NIV)*
Life Principle	Trust must be earned. Since no human is perfect, failure is certain. So why trust in yourself? Trust in God, who alone is perfect in love, power and wisdom.
Life changes	_____ _____ _____ _____ _____ _____ _____ _____ ⇨ ∞ 💭 ◁ ⌂ ⊕ 🎯

November 28

God's Word	A man who remains stiff-necked after many rebukes will suddenly be destroyed—without remedy. (Proverbs 29:1, NIV)
Life Principle	There is an old proverb: *If three friends tell you that you are drunk, you should go lie down.* Refusing to listen to wise counsel puts your own life in danger.
Life changes	_____ _____ _____ _____ _____ _____ _____ _____

November 29

God's Word	*A man who loves wisdom brings joy to his father, but a companion of prostitutes squanders his wealth.* *(Proverbs 29:3, NIV)*
Life Principle	Sexual favors are tempting, expensive, and unwise. God, in His wisdom, gave the sexual union as a gift to mankind – but only in the context of marriage.
Life changes	_____ _____ _____ _____ _____ _____ _____ _____

November 30

God's Word	*By justice a king gives a country stability, but one who is greedy for bribes tears it down.* *(Proverbs 29:4, NIV)*
Life Principle	The wheels of justice may turn slowly but it beats the alternative. No one wins when lawlessness prevails.
Life changes	

December

The proverbs of Solomon
son of David, king of Israel: ... for
understanding proverbs and parables,
the sayings and riddles of the wise.
(Proverbs 1:1,5, NIV)

Symbol	Life Change
⇨	A command to follow
∞	A principle to use
💭?	Thoughts to engage and attitudes to avoid
📢	What you say and how you say it
⚒	A good work to start
✛	A sin to confess and forsake
🎯	Thanksgiving for God's hand at work in your life

December 1

God's Word	*An evil man is snared by his own sin, but a righteous one can sing and be glad. (Proverbs 29:6, NIV)*
Life Principle	Sin is a trap, a burden you were never intended to bear. That is why Jesus paid for your sin on the cross. Repent and believe so you too can sing and be glad.
Life changes	_____ _____ _____ _____ _____ _____ _____ _____

December 2

God's Word	*Mockers stir up a city, but wise men turn away anger. (Proverbs 29:8, NIV)*
Life Principle	When a fire is raging, you must cut off its fuel supply. A peacemaker finds a way to calm people down and give them perspective.
Life changes	_____ _____ _____ _____ _____ _____ _____ _____

December 3

God's Word	*Bloodthirsty men hate a man of integrity and seek to kill the upright.* *(Proverbs 29:10, NIV)*
Life Principle	Why hate an honest man? You hate honesty because you: do not want to hear the truth, do not want to be confused by the facts, do not want your sin exposed.
Life changes	_____ _____ _____ _____ _____ _____ _____ _____

December 4

God's Word	A fool gives full vent to his anger, but a wise man keeps himself under control. (Proverbs 29:11, NIV)
Life Principle	Unbridled anger has hurt more people than all the wars combined. Self-control is a gift from God to those who surrender to His will and His wisdom.
Life changes	_____ _____ _____ _____ _____ _____ _____

December 5

God's Word	*If a ruler listens to lies, all his officials become wicked. (Proverbs 29:12, NIV)*
Life Principle	Integrity and accountability are vital for anyone in a leadership position. Even small moral failures will spread quickly: *If the leader does it, it must be OK…*
Life changes	_____ _____ _____ _____ _____ _____ _____ _____

December 6

God's Word	*The poor man and the oppressor have this in common: The LORD gives sight to the eyes of both. (Proverbs 29:13, NIV)*
Life Principle	Why is God so gracious that He would show kindness to both the deserving and undeserving? Because God created you. That makes you very special.
Life changes	_____ _____ _____ _____ _____ _____ _____ _____

December 7

God's Word	*Discipline your son, and he will give you peace; he will bring delight to your soul. (Proverbs 29:17, NIV)*
Life Principle	Discipline is not simply punishment – it involves teaching and correcting. Children need to be guided along a righteous path – it is not the natural course.
Life changes	_____ _____ _____ _____ _____ _____ _____ _____ ⇨ ∞ 💬 📢 ⌂ ⊕ ⦿

December 8

God's Word	*Where there is no revelation, the people cast off restraint; but blessed is he who keeps the law.* *(Proverbs 29:18, NIV)*
Life Principle	If you had no knowledge of God's word, no knowledge of God's standard, would you be a person of higher or lower virtue?
Life changes	_____ _____ _____ _____ _____ _____ _____

December 9

God's Word	Do you see a man who speaks in haste? There is more hope for a fool than for him. (Proverbs 29:20, NIV)
Life Principle	Though your mouth is less than an inch in front of your brain, it can run miles ahead. Slow down and think before you speak.
Life changes	_____ _____ _____ _____ _____ _____ _____ _____

SPEEDY DEVOTIONS (VOLUME 1)

December 10

God's Word	*An angry man stirs up dissension, and a hot-tempered one commits many sins.* *(Proverbs 29:22, NIV)*
Life Principle	Try to stir up trouble and act righteously at the same time. It cannot happen.
Life changes	_____ _____ _____ _____ _____ _____ _____ ⇨ ∞ 💭 📢 🔥 ⊕ 🎯

December 11

God's Word	*A man's pride brings him low, but a man of lowly spirit gains honor.* *(Proverbs 29:23, NIV)*
Life Principle	The way *up* leads *down* and the way *down* leads *up*. In man's economy, the opposite is true. Since God is God and you are not, which is the winning way?
Life changes	_____ _____ _____ _____ _____ _____ _____

December 12

God's Word	Fear of man will prove to be a snare, but whoever trusts in the LORD is kept safe. (Proverbs 29:25, NIV)
Life Principle	People can be intimidating and life can be over-whelming. But Jesus said, "surely I am with you always." (Matthew 28:20, NIV)
Life changes	_____ _____ _____ _____ _____ _____ _____ _____

December 13

God's Word	*The righteous detest the dishonest; the wicked detest the upright.* *(Proverbs 29:27, NIV)*
Life Principle	There are big differences in the principles of those who trust in the LORD and those who do not. But remember the battle is not against people but for the truth.
Life changes	_____ _____ _____ _____ _____ _____ _____

December 14

God's Word	*Every word of God is flawless; he is a shield to those who take refuge in him.* *(Proverbs 30:5, NIV)*
Life Principle	The world says, "*Look before you leap*" but "*He who hesitates is lost.*" Which is it? The only firm foundation in life is the clear, unchanging word of God.
Life changes	_____ _____ _____ _____ _____ _____ _____

December 15

God's Word	*Keep falsehood and lies far from me; give me neither poverty nor riches, but give me only my daily bread. (Proverbs 30:8, NIV)*
Life Principle	Poverty is bad. Wealth is good. But the best is to have just enough. Seek the LORD's path and He will provide you enough for each day.
Life changes	_____ _____ _____ _____ _____ _____ _____ _____

December 16

God's Word	Do not slander a servant to his master, or he will curse you, and you will pay for it. (Proverbs 30:10, NIV)
Life Principle	It is tempting to compare your work to others. This only leads to ill will. Strive to please the LORD with your work and you will not have to worry about others.
Life changes	_____ _____ _____ _____ _____ _____ _____ _____

December 17

God's Word	*The leech has two daughters. 'Give! Give!' they cry. (Proverbs 30:15, NIV)*
Life Principle	The Bible tells us that love never demands its own way. Instead, love works hard to meet the genuine needs of others.
Life changes	_____ _____ _____ _____ _____ _____ _____ _____

December 18

God's Word	*The eye that mocks a father, that scorns obedience to a mother, will be pecked out by the ravens of the valley. (Proverbs 30:17, NIV)*
Life Principle	These are strong words because the issue is so important: the family unit is the foundation of a viable society. Honor your parents who raised you.
Life changes	_____ _____ _____ _____ _____ _____ _____ ⇨ ∞ 💭 📢 🙌 ⊕ 🎯

December 19

God's Word	*This is the way of an adulteress: She eats and wipes her mouth and says, 'I've done nothing wrong.' (Proverbs 30:20, NIV)*
Life Principle	Shame has been all but eliminated from our culture. But shame, because of wicked actions, will lead to accountability. In the end, everyone benefits.
Life changes	_____ _____ _____ _____ _____ _____ _____ ⇨ ∞ 💭 📢 ⛏ ⊕ 🎯

December 20

God's Word	*Ants are creatures of little strength, yet they store up their food in the summer; (Proverbs 30:25, NIV)*
Life Principle	Work while you can and save all you can. You never know when your can will be empty.
Life changes	

December 21

God's Word	*O my son, ... do not spend your strength on women, your vigor on those who ruin kings.* *(Proverbs 31:2-3, NIV)*
Life Principle	Sexual sin is the downfall of people great and small. Strive for greatness by being pure and faithful to the one you love.
Life changes	_____ _____ _____ _____ _____ _____ _____ _____ ⇨ ∞ 💬 📢 ⌂ ⊕ 🎯

December 22

God's Word	*It is not for kings ... to drink wine, ... to crave beer, lest they ... forget what the law decrees, and deprive all the oppressed of their rights.* (Proverbs 31:4-5, NIV)
Life Principle	Too much alcohol will make you say and do things you will regret – and so will the innocent people you hurt.
Life changes	_____ _____ _____ _____ _____ _____ _____ _____

December 23

God's Word	*Speak up for those who cannot speak for themselves, for the rights of all who are destitute.* *(Proverbs 31:8, NIV)*
Life Principle	Do you look at the destitute and say, "I am glad that is not me!" Or do you think, "That is not my problem!" Do what you can for those who cannot.
Life changes	_____ _____ _____ _____ _____ _____ _____

December 24

God's Word	A wife of noble character who can find? She is worth far more than rubies. (Proverbs 31:10, NIV)
Life Principle	A noble character is to be greatly desired more than all the money in the world. Riches will never make you wise, loving, or patient.
Life changes	_____ _____ _____ _____ _____ _____ _____ _____

December 25

God's Word	*A wife of noble character … She brings him good, not harm, all the days of her life. (Proverbs 31:10,12, NIV)*
Life Principle	Noble character brings what is good for others to others. The greatest good was brought to you by the LORD on the 1st Christmas: Jesus, the Savior of the world.
Life changes	_____ _____ _____ _____ _____ _____ _____ _____ ⇨ ∞ 💭 📢 ⏏ ⊕ 🎯

December 26

God's Word	*A wife of noble character ... She gets up while it is still dark; she provides food for her family ... (Proverbs 31:10,15, NIV)*
Life Principle	Noble character works hard. Yes, work is hard. That is why it is called *work* and not *play*. But your purpose is clear: to support yourself and your family.
Life changes	_____ _____ _____ _____ _____ _____ _____ ⇨ ∞ 💭 📢 ☝ ⊕ 🎯

December 27

God's Word	*A wife of noble character ... She sets about her work vigorously; her arms are strong for her tasks. (Proverbs 31:10,17, NIV)*
Life Principle	Noble character works with enthusiasm. No boss ever commends a worker who only gives the minimum required to get paid.
Life changes	_____ _____ _____ _____ _____ _____ _____ _____

December 28

God's Word	*A wife of noble character ... She opens her arms to the poor and extends her hands to the needy.* *(Proverbs 31:10,20, NIV)*
Life Principle	Noble character is generous to a fault. To give, the Bible says, brings the giver more blessings than the recipient (Acts 20:35).
Life changes	_____ _____ _____ _____ _____ _____ _____

December 29

God's Word	*A wife of noble character ... Her husband is respected at the city gate, where he takes his seat among the elders of the land.* *(Proverbs 31:10,23, NIV)*
Life Principle	Noble character gives everyone the respect due them. Every human being is made in God's image and deserving of basic decency and kindness.
Life changes	_____ _____ _____ _____ _____ _____ _____ _____

December 30

God's Word	*A wife of noble character ... She watches over the affairs of her household and does not eat the bread of idleness. (Proverbs 31:10,27, NIV)*
Life Principle	Noble character keeps a close eye on relationships. Like two rafts afloat in the ocean, any relationship is either drawing closer together or drifting apart.
Life changes	_____ _____ _____ _____ _____ _____ _____

December 31

God's Word	*Charm is deceptive, and beauty is fleeting; but a woman who fears the LORD is to be praised.* *(Proverbs 31:30, NIV)*
Life Principle	Physical beauty will not last no matter how many operations you receive. Yet you are always beautiful on the inside when you trust and obey the LORD.
Life changes	_____ _____ _____ _____ _____ _____ _____

A Personal Relationship With God

The most wonderful relationship you can ever have is with the One who loves you so very much that He brought you into existence. God is your Creator[1] and He desperately wants you to know Him as He knows you.[2] Can you truly say that you have a personal relationship with God? If not, these next few pages will help you to start a relationship with God that will last for time and eternity.

---

[1] *In the beginning, God created the heavens and the earth. (Genesis 1:1, NIV)*

First, you must acknowledge that God is God and you are not. I know, you do not think you are an all-powerful being who can command things into existence. What I mean is that God is God and you do not live your life on your terms but on His terms. After all, if God is God, then He created the world in which you live. If you want to be right with God and live well in His creation, then you must submit to His rule and authority over your life.

Why does that seem so hard? From the very beginning, the first man and woman chose to live life on their own terms.[3] And every human being since has

---

[2] *You will seek me and find me when you seek me with all your heart. (Jeremiah 29:13, NIV)*
[3] *Genesis 3:1-19. God made Adam and Eve without sin but with the ability to make choices. Each of them chose to disobey God's one command to them.*

chosen the same path.[4] We want what we want when we want it - usually without regard to the consequences. The Bible calls this sin.[5] God is perfect and has a perfect standard of righteousness. When we try to live apart from God, we cross over the line of righteousness into sin. This tendency toward selfishness is part of our inner being. It is why we cannot feel right with God – because God is holy and we are not.

The good news is that God desires to have a relationship with you anyway. He has done everything necessary for you to enter into a right relationship with Him:

- God stepped out of heaven and became a real human being –

---

[4] *Romans 5:12. Adam, the first man, is the father of all human beings.*
[5] *There is no difference, for all have sinned and fall short of the glory of God. (Romans 3:22-23, NIV)*

without the sinful nature that we have. This is Jesus.[6]

- He lived the perfect life that you and I can never live.[7]

- Jesus offered His perfect life on a cross to pay the penalty for your sins – and for the sins of everyone in the world.[8]

- He rose from the dead so you can know that He is LORD, His sacrifice was acceptable, and that your sins are forgiven.[9]

If you will trust in Jesus as LORD of your life and believe His death on the cross paid for your sins, you will be forgiven and

---

[6] *In the beginning was the Word [Jesus], and the Word was with God, and the Word was God ... The Word became flesh and made his dwelling among us. (John 1:1,14, NIV)*
[7] *God made him [Jesus] who had no sin to be a sin offering for us, so that in him we might become the righteousness of God. (2 Corinthians 5:21, NIV)*
[8] *For Christ died for sins once for all, the righteous for the unrighteous, to bring you to God. (1 Peter 3:18, NIV)*
[9] *... for us who believe in him who raised Jesus our Lord from the dead. He was delivered over to death for our sins and was raised to life for our justification. (Romans 4:23-25, NIV)*

given eternal life.[10] Eternal life is not some wispy existence as an angel sitting on a cloud strumming a harp. Eternal life is a forever relationship with God that starts the moment you choose to believe.

God loves you because He created you – you belong to Him.[11] Will you accept His grace and forgiveness and enter into a loving relationship with your Creator? If this is your desire, you can pray to the LORD right now. You can use the words of this prayer to help you in this first step. The power is not in the words themselves

---

[10] *That if you confess with your mouth, "Jesus is Lord," and believe in your heart that God raised him from the dead, you will be saved. For it is with your heart that you believe and are justified, and it is with your mouth that you confess and are saved. (Romans 10:9-10, NIV)*
[11] *For God so loved the world that he gave his one and only Son,[Jesus] that whoever believes in him shall not perish but have eternal life. For God did not send his Son into the world to condemn the world, but to save the world through him. (John 3:16-17, NIV)*

but in your agreement with them and belief in the God who made you:

> *Dear LORD Jesus - thank You for never giving up on me. I want to have a loving relationship with You. Please forgive me – not because I deserve it but because You died on a cross for my sins. Since You rose from the dead, I put my faith and trust in You and will begin to follow you because you are LORD. Thank you for giving me eternal life and hope. Amen.*

If you prayed in earnest, you should be filled with the joy of knowing God and being in a right relationship with Him. The Bible says, *"Yet to all who received him, to those who believed in his name, he gave the right to become children of God"* (John 1:12, *NIV*). Welcome to God's family – forever!

About the Author

Randy Lariscy is an author, evangelist, and Bible Teacher. He is a bivocational minister, licensed at Roswell Street Baptist church and ordained at Noonday Baptist Church in Marietta, Georgia. Working in both business and ministry vocations has provided Randy with unique set of skills which he uses for God's glory and to further His kingdom.

His various roles in ministry have included:

- Evangelism Consultant
- Education Pastor

- Supply Preacher
- Radio Bible Teacher

He holds a Master of Arts in Pastoral Ministry from Trinity Theological Seminary and a Master of Divinity. He has been married for over 30 years to Mary, a registered nurse, and they have two adult children and one grandchild. They reside in Kennesaw, Georgia.

WordTruth Press^{SM}

Quality resources with significant spiritual impact

Look for more great resources from WordTruth Press:

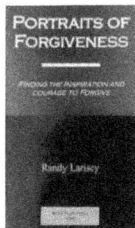

	Portraits of Forgiveness Finding the Inspiration and Courage to Forgive
PORTRAITS OF FORGIVENESS *FINDING THE INSPIRATION AND COURAGE TO FORGIVE* Randy Lansey *Available now* *$9.95 USD*	Like an old, frayed blanket there are many loose threads in our relationships. Issues and conflict divide us from family, friends, and innumerable people we encounter throughout life. The

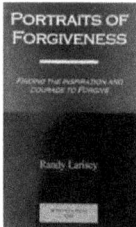 **PORTRAITS OF FORGIVENESS** *FINDING THE INSPIRATION AND COURAGE TO FORGIVE* Randy Lariscy *Available now* *$9.95 USD*	process of forgiveness is necessary to restore and rebuild those relationships. In this book you will find great stories of how God works in the lives of people to bring about forgiveness and reconciliation - binding up the loose threads and making relationships even stronger than before.
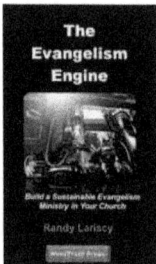 **The Evangelism Engine** *Build a Sustainable Evangelism Ministry in Your Church* Randy Lariscy WindTrust Press *Targeted for release in 2013*	**The Evangelism Engine** Build a Sustainable Evangelism Ministry in Your Church Evangelism is a ministry of the church that usually runs hot or cold depending on the passion and energy of one person in the church. The Evangelism Engine enables churches to establish evangelism as a sustainable, long-term process. This book targets church pastors and ministry leaders.

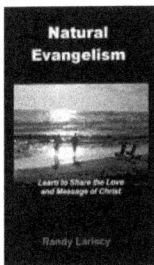Targeted for release in 2013	**Natural Evangelism** Learn to Share the Love and Message of Christ Natural Evangelism helps individual believers under-stand and embrace the call to be a disciple-making disciple. This practical train-ing covers multiple approa-ches to sharing the good news of God's grace, techni-ques for visiting with people, and how to find prospects for the kingdom of God.
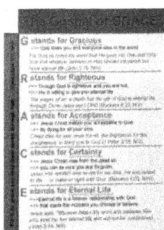$9.95 USD Qty 50	**The Gospel of GRACE** Evangelism Tract (Qty 50) This attractive 3x5 card presents the good news using the word GRACE as an acrostic. Each letter represents a different aspect of God's grace at work in salvation. Glossy, color front and black-and-white back.

	The Ten Commandments *Evangelism Tract (Qty 50)*
The Ten Commandments $9.95 USD Qty 50	The Ten Commandments are shown on the front of this 3x5 card with a positive version of each command. On the back is a presentation of the gospel. It is printed with a glossy, color front and black-and-white back.

The mission of WordTruth Press is to provide quality Bible-based resources with significant spiritual impact for individuals and churches. Education and evangelism are the main focus of WordTruth Press. Following the Great Commission of the LORD Jesus (Matthew 28:18-20), this organization provides Bible-based resources to evangelize the world, encourage and equip believers and churches for evangelism, and provide solid Bible teaching to build up the body of Christ.

A key strategy is to find low-cost channels for production and distribution to maximize the availability of our resources to people around the world. WordTruth Press also offers many free resources for churches and individuals available online at:

www.WordTruth.com

www.ingramcontent.com/pod-product-compliance
Lightning Source LLC
Chambersburg PA
CBHW031824090426
42741CB00005B/116